# Decorative
# PAINT
# &FAUX FINISHES

By The Editors of Sunset Books

SUNSET BOOKS
Menlo Park, CA

**Sunset Books**

Vice President, General Manager: Richard A. Smeby

Editorial Director: Bob Doyle

Production Director: Lory Day

Art Director: Vasken Guiragossian

*Decorative Paint & Faux Finishes* was produced in conjunction with Roundtable Press, Inc.

Directors: Marsha Melnick, Susan E. Meyer, Julie Merberg

**Staff for this book:**

Developmental Editor: Linda J. Selden

Senior Editor: Carol Spier

Decorative Painter and Consultant: Justina Jorrin Barnard, Peinture Decorative, New York City

Step-by-Step Photography: Steven Mays Photography

Book Design: Areta Buk/Thumb Print

Technical Writer: Diane O'Connell

Copy Editor: Virginia Croft

Illustrations: Beverley Bozarth Colgan

Photo Research: Ede Rothaus

Assistant Editor: John Glenn

Production Assistant: Patricia S. Williams

Cover: Faux painting by Shari Steele Designs, Palo Alto, CA. Wall courtesy of St. Michael's Alley Restaurant, Palo Alto, CA. Cover design by Vasken Guiragossian. Photography by Philip Harvey and E. Andrew McKinney. Photo direction by JoAnn Masaoka Van Atta. Additional photography acknowledgments appear on page 176.

*15 14*

First printing September 1999

ISBN 0-376-01388-5

Library of Congress Catalog Card Number: 99-63572

Printed in China.

For additional copies of *Decorative Paint & Faux Finishes* or any other *Sunset* book, call 1-800-526-5111. Or see our Web site at www.sunsetbooks.com

# FOREWORD

Walls are the blank canvas of our homes, an open invitation to embellishment. With the addition of color and pattern, walls assume character and set the tone for our decor—light, bright, subdued, lively, imposing, subtle, or exuberant, as we wish. With the imaginative use of paint, anyone can transform a plain expanse of wallboard into a decorative backdrop, choosing options that range from demure and barely perceptible washes of color to bold figurative or geometric patterns.

*Decorative Paint & Faux Finishes* will inspire and teach you to do more than forty painting techniques. Divided in two sections, Basics and Techniques, it's filled with ideas for using color and pattern, has easy-to-follow directions, and provides a solid technical background for selecting and using the necessary materials and tools. And everything in this book can be done using readily available paints and equipment—in many cases with everyday house paint or ready-mixed glazes and inexpensive brushes.

As you turn the pages of this book, you'll see directions for numerous painted finishes for walls and woodwork, each illustrated with step-by-step as well as inspirational interior photographs. To begin, browse to see which painted effects most appeal to you, and skim the directions to get an idea of the painting processes. Many of the techniques are easy to do—and easy to adapt and combine. With this book in hand you'll be able to reproduce paint effects featured in design magazines, or come up with original variations uniquely suited to your home.

Before you go beyond the browsing stage, read the first section of the book, Basics. Even though you don't need to be an art school graduate to undertake attractive decorative painting, you do need to understand the properties of the different types of paint. In Basics you'll find a thorough discussion of paints and painting tools. Basics concludes with an overview of color theory, which you'll find especially helpful when planning a palette.

Note also the Tricks of the Trade inserted throughout the book. These special features clarify often puzzling parts of the painting process, such as what to do in corners or how to hold different brushes to achieve specific effects. They provide information for planning and setting up the more complex or geometric techniques—invaluable if you wish to paint stripes or space a stencil at regular intervals. If you'd like to paint a mural, you'll see how to transfer a design to the wall, and can even learn a bit about perspective drawing and trompe l'oeil modeling. Pages with Tricks of the Trade have colored borders, so you can recognize them at a glance.

The techniques and processes featured in this book are explained for working on walls, floors, woodwork, or other architectural elements, but many of them can be used on furniture or accessories as well. In fact, if you wish to learn Gilding, Wood Graining, or one of the faux stone finishes, a small project such as a box or picture frame is the perfect place to begin.

If you are a novice painter and feel somewhat insecure, relax. While imagination and artistic talent are wonderful assets for anyone wanting to do decorative painting, they are not prerequisites. Having the proper materials and tools and taking the time to plan and practice your chosen technique are far more important. Even some of the seemingly complex faux finishes can be very successfully painted by beginners, though others do require more skill and familiarity with art supplies. Most of the painting effects can be interpreted in many ways, one being no more "right" than another, especially if you like the way it looks. The biggest mistake you are likely to make is to underestimate the amount of time needed to paint an entire room. So think through your project, test and practice to be sure you understand the technique and like the way the colors work together, and then have fun.

# CONTENTS

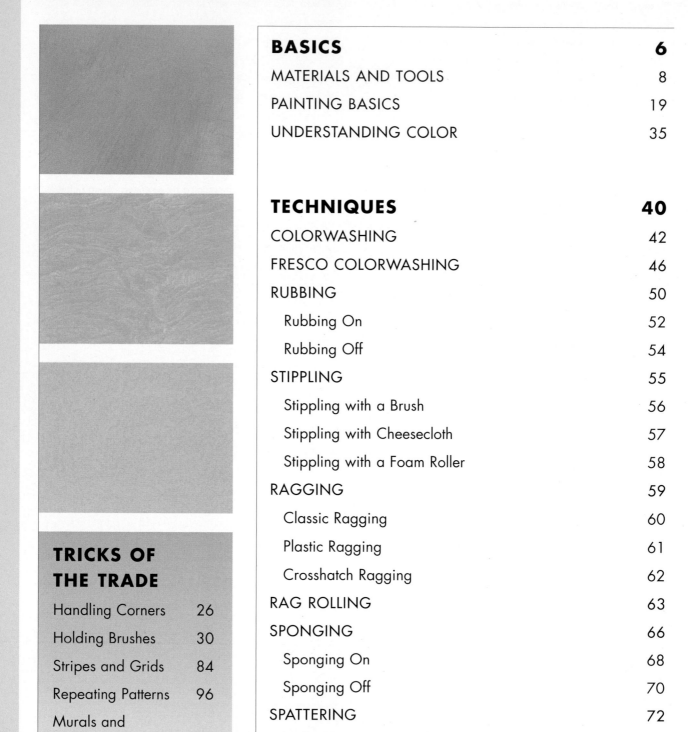

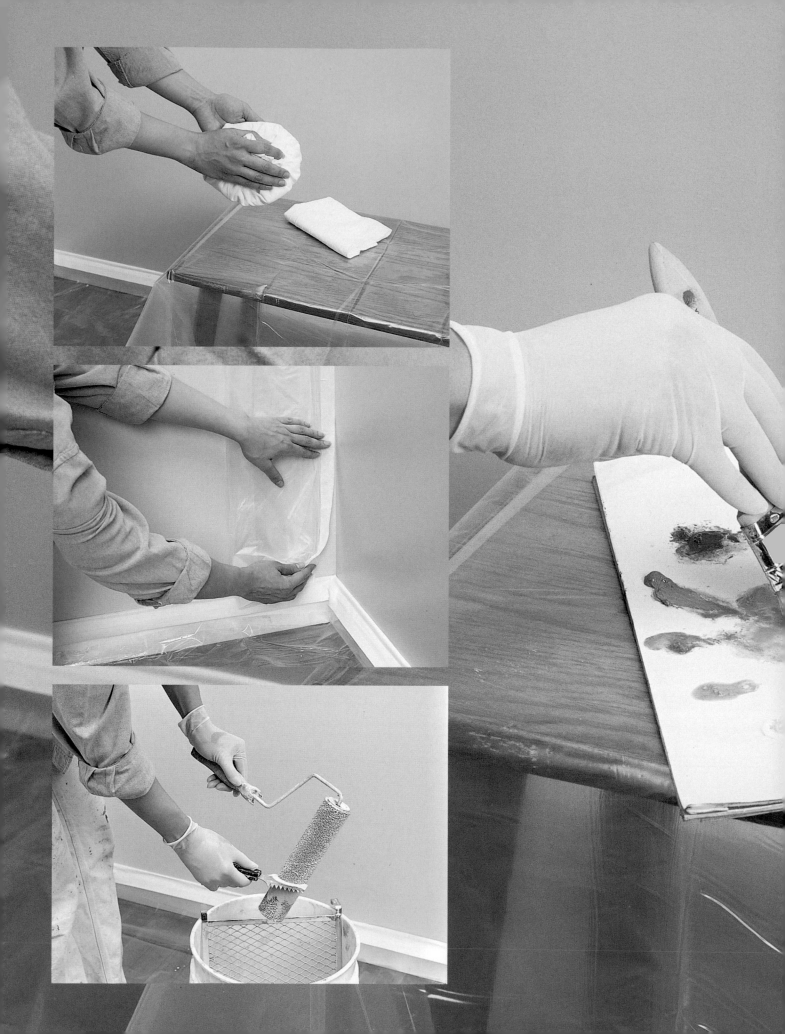

If you are looking through this book, you are no doubt thinking about using decorative painting in your home and wondering how to go about it. Most of us have done some house painting of one sort or another, and we're not especially daunted by it. Decorative painting uses the same basic skills and materials in combination with a few fine art techniques and mediums. Once you are familiar with these, the process is fun and creative. This chapter provides the background information you'll need to do any of the techniques featured in this book.

The first section, Materials and Tools, is an introduction to the paints, mediums, and equipment that are used. You'll learn about the different properties of oil- and water-base paints and find basic recipes for mixing decorative glazes. You'll see which brushes, tools, and general equipment are always needed and which are for special processes.

In the section Painting Basics, you'll learn how to handle the equipment and the ways in which house painting and decorative painting are the same and how they differ. You'll learn about the importance of surface preparation and the correct method for applying the base coat of paint. You'll also find important information on cleanup and safe handling of volatile materials.

The final section, Understanding Color, explains the basics of color theory, which you'll find useful when you are choosing the hues for your base paint and glaze.

Whether you are a novice or an experienced painter, read this chapter. Many painters use the same terms to mean different things; it is important that you understand these terms as they are used in this book.

# MATERIALS AND TOOLS

To a novice, decorative painting can seem mysterious, dependent upon an array of exotic brushes and skilled handwork. While it is true that some faux finishing techniques can take years to perfect, many painted effects can be very successfully executed with everyday tools by anyone with the patience to read directions and practice them to gain familiarity with the materials and processes. An understanding of the tools and paints used will make the work go smoothly and save time and money. And the appropriate general equipment will ensure that your workspace is neat, efficient, and safe.

## ABOUT PAINTING TOOLS

Although there are numerous specialty brushes and rollers available for decorative painting, you really don't need many of them for the techniques featured in this book. The samples shown were all painted with the tools specified in the directions, so use the materials lists as a guide when you assemble the gear for your chosen technique. Don't hesitate to work with the inexpensive chip and foam brushes that are frequently specified, but when house painter's, artist's, or specialty brushes are called for, use the best quality you can afford. Ask your vendor for advice if you are unsure about what to purchase.

### PAINT ROLLERS

Look for a roller with a heavy-gauge steel frame, an expandable wire cage, and a comfortable handle threaded with a metal sleeve to accommodate an extension pole. A 9" roller is appropriate for nearly all jobs.

• Choose a roller cover appropriate for the paint you're using. Use a nylon cover for latex paint. Nylon and wool blend, lambskin, and mohair covers are recommended for alkyd paint. Nap thickness on roller covers varies from $1/16$" to $1^1/4$". The smoother the surface you're painting, the shorter the nap you should use.
• For decorative techniques, you'll most often use a 9" low-nap roller or a foam hot-dog roller (named for its shape).
• There is also a variety of special rollers (and their relatives— rocking tools and novelty graining pads) with textured or raised-pattern surfaces. These are readily available in paint and art supply stores. Depending upon the type, they can be used to create mock rag-rolled patterns, fantasy wood grain on walls and flat doors, quasi-realistic wood grain on floorboards, or various imaginative allover patterns. But beware: while they look intriguing they can be frustrating to use. You can't reroll glaze with a textured tool, and it's nearly impossible to align adjacent passes or correct imperfections. So experiment with these tools to see what they do. You might want to reserve them for use on small items or defined areas, such as floorboards or door components. See Novelty Tools, page 136.

## PAINTBRUSHES

Good-quality brushes perform very differently from less expensive ones. A good brush is well balanced, holds a lot of paint, and puts the paint where you want it. A good brush almost always features long bristles firmly set into an easy-to-grip wood handle. There are times when lesser-quality brushes will do, and even worn brushes are useful for some hand-painted details, but in general, you should buy the best quality you can afford.

• Natural bristle brushes should be used to apply alkyd paint and other finishes that clean up with paint thinner. Don't use them for applying latex paint and other water-base products, because the bristles become limp when they soak up the water in the base.
• Synthetic filament brushes should be used to apply latex paint. Polyester brushes remain sturdy in water, keeping their shape for detail work. A good-quality synthetic brush can also be used with alkyd paint.
• Foam brushes are handy for small jobs and quick touch-ups and are used in many of the decorative techniques. They're disposable, but if you're bothered by the idea of pitching them into the landfill, use a bristle brush instead and clean it properly.

## DECORATIVE PAINTING TOOLS

Most of the techniques explained in this book can be painted using a few simple and widely available tools. A few techniques require more specialized tools, but even these are commonly stocked by good paint vendors. The following tools are pictured on pages 10–11.

**Artist's brushes** Artist's brushes are essential for many faux finishes, for adding details to Stenciling, and for touching up. You'll need a variety of flat, round, and angled brushes in sizes up to about 1" wide or 1" in diameter, as well as very fine touch-up (watercolor) brushes. Script liners and fan brushes are used for Graining. Use worn or inexpensive artist's brushes to mix glazes.

**Burlap** Burlap is used to make veins for faux Mahogany.

**Cheesecloth** Cheesecloth can be used to stipple or rub glazes. It is packaged precut, which is handy, and in continuous lengths.

**Chip brushes** Inexpensive and versatile, chip brushes are used to apply glaze as well as to soften—and they're much cheaper than the badger hair softener traditionally used in faux finishing. You can also use them to apply glaze to moldings.

**Cosmetic sponges** Small, fine sponges are useful for applying a small-scale soft pattern, especially when stenciling.

**Eraser tools** Also called color shapers, these angled erasers in paintbrush-like handles are available in several sizes. They are good for removing fine lines of glaze in Wood Graining, Malachite, or Vinegar Painting.

**Feathers** Turkey feathers can be used for fantasy graining and novelty effects and for manipulating vinegar glazes.

**Flogger** A long-bristled horsehair brush used to create "pores" in Wood Graining, this brush is somewhat expensive. You can also flog with a standard house painter's brush.

**Foam brushes** Cheap, disposable foam brushes are ideal for a variety of uses, from touching up spots to cutting in glaze to glazing small surfaces for faux finishing techniques.

**Graining combs** Used for Combing and fantasy Wood Graining, graining combs come with rubber or metal teeth. Each creates a different pattern in a different scale. Shown on pages 10–11 are two small rubber combs (#28), one with graduated teeth, and two wide wooden combs with rubber teeth (#30).

**House painter's brushes** Several sizes of house painter's brushes are essential: a thickly bristled 4" brush for spreading paint on larger surfaces; a 2" or 3" brush for painting woodwork; and a 1" angled sash brush for cutting in corners and detail work (such as window muntins). House painter's brushes of any width can also be used for softening in decorative painting.

**Jersey rags** Knit rags are used to rub glazes. Paint stores carry them packaged in plastic bags or 5-pound boxes; buy the jersey (smooth knit), not the ribbed, variety.

**Mottler** This small square brush is used for applying metal leaf.

**Narrow masking tape** Skinny $1/16$" to $1/4$" masking or drafting tape is used to mask grout or inlay lines in stone block or tile patterns. Tape narrower than $1/4$" is difficult to find, but a good office supply store can order it for you if they don't stock it.

**Novelty graining tools** Novelty rubber graining tools come in various patterns and scales, sometimes with handles. Not pictured, but also useful, are synthetic floor scrub pads and steel wool, both of which can be used to create fine dragged patterns.

**Paper towels** Paper towels (not shown) are invaluable. Use good-quality absorbent paper towels to manipulate glazes and to blot or wipe paint-laden tools.

**Rubber stamps** Available at craft and stationery stores, stamps can be used with glazes, alone, or over other painted techniques.

**Sea sponges** Natural sponges are used for Sponging and to paint Limestone and Granite. The larger the pores and more jagged the edges, the more open the painted impression will be.

**Softener** A badger hair brush is used to mute (soften) overall effects, such as Colorwashing, or details, such as veins in graining.

**Stippling brush** This brush, made with hog hair or horsehair bristles imbedded in a large ferrule/handle, is designed to be pounced (tapped) rather than brushed over a surface. Used specifically to remove glaze, it is an expensive but worthwhile tool if you are stippling a large area. Several sizes are available.

**Stencil brushes** Cylindrical brushes made with hog hair bristles and blunt cut are used to pounce or swirl paint onto a surface through a stencil. Their handles are usually short, though European stencil brushes are sometimes long-handled.

**Veiner** The veiner is a long-haired natural bristle brush used to create veins for Wood Graining and Marble.

In addition to the brushes and other tools used to manipulate the glazes, you'll need some basic painting and protective equipment. The following can be purchased in hardware stores and paint stores.

**Artist's palette and palette knife** Use an artist's palette and palette knife when working with artist's paints. Disposable palette pads are inexpensive and don't require the cleaning of a costlier wood palette. Just be sure the paper leaves have a shiny surface. (See pages 10–11 and 17.)

**Bucket and rack** A 5-gallon bucket fitted with a metal roller grid is the best container for primer or base coat paint for a large area.

**Curved painter's tool** This handy tool has a crescent blade for scraping excess glaze off a roller. It can also be used to open paint cans and scrape inside corners. One style has a toothed edge for combing bristles in addition to the curved edge.

**Drop cloths** These are available in paper, plastic, and canvas. Canvas is the best, but it's expensive and cumbersome. Plastic can be slippery. Paper won't protect against spilled paint.

**Edge guide** This handy device offers quick, portable protection for floors and carpets when you're painting baseboards.

**Labeling system** For labeling mixed glazes and mediums, have 1" masking tape and a permanent marker handy.

**Measuring devices** For measuring and marking, a variety of rulers, tape measures, chalk lines, blackboard chalk, and pencils should be on hand.

**Mixing containers and stir sticks** When preparing or storing glazes, you'll need assorted clean mixing containers (with lids) for storage and myriad stir sticks.

**Paint tray** A paint tray is the best container for glazes that are to be rolled on. Disposable liners make cleanup easier.

**Painter's masking tape** Masking tape in several types is invaluable. Brown paper painter's masking tape has one sticky edge; it provides inexpensive all-purpose protection for adjacent surfaces. Blue masking tape is good for masking delicate surfaces and hardware and is less likely to remove paint; it is rather costly, so reserve it for special situations.

**Plumb bobs** These homemade weighted guides are used for dragging or combing straight lines. (See pages 10–11 and 12.)

**Rubber gloves** Wear gloves to protect your skin from chemicals. Disposable nonsterile latex gloves (available from a pharmacy or beauty supply store) allow flexible movement but wear out quickly. Heavy-duty rubber work gloves are fine for techniques that don't require delicate handwork and for cleanup.

**Sandpaper and tack cloth** Always have fine sandpaper, a sanding block, and a tack cloth ready to smooth surfaces between coats of paint or glaze.

**Stepladder** A sturdy ladder is necessary for almost any project involving walls or ceilings.

# GLAZING TOOLS

1  Turkey feathers
2  Rubber stamps
3  Stencil brushes
4  Plumb bob
Artist's brushes:
  5  $1/2$" flat brush
  6  $3/16$" round brush
  7  $1/4$" worn-down brush
  8  $1/4$" angled brush
  9  $1/4$" round synthetic sable brush
  10  Eraser tool
  11  $1/8$" round synthetic sable brush
  12  Touch-up brushes
  13  Script liner
14  Palette knife
15  Jersey rag
16  Cosmetic sponges
17  Sea sponge
18  Cheesecloth
19  Chip brush with cut bristles
20  Burlap scrap

21  Brown paper painter's masking tape
22  Narrow masking tape
23  Chip brush
24  House painter's brush
25  Mixing brushes
26  Foam brush
27  Foam hot-dog roller
28  Graining combs
29  Novelty graining tools
30  Graining combs
31  Stir sticks
32  Fan brush
33  Veiner
34  Mottler
35  Softeners
36  Stippling brush
37  Flogger

Some of the decorative techniques call for you to fashion your own tools. Here are directions for making two that you'll find used repeatedly.

### PLUMB BOBS

Plumb bobs are used as guides for painting straight vertical lines in techniques such as Dragging and Combing.

Cut a length of mason's twine or heavy string equal to the height of the wall plus a few inches. Cut as many as needed to place at 2' intervals along the wall. Tie a washer to one end of each length of twine. Tape the other end of each length to the ceiling about 3" in front of the wall so the washer hangs free (see the photo on pages 10–11).

### BOLSTER RAGS

Bolster rags, made from jersey rags or cheesecloth, are used to rub and stipple glazes.

**1** Flatten several rags and then fold each to be about 6" square and stack them.

**2** Center the stack on another flattened, unfolded rag. Wrap the flattened rag around the folded rags and wad and grasp the excess in your working hand. As you work, you can rearrange the wrapping until it is too soiled to be of further use, then change it.

If you want to make your own stencil, first work out the design on paper, including the way it will repeat once in each appropriate direction. Use a photocopier to speed the task. On the final sketch, mark lines to delineate the edges of the central repeat. Then mark lines parallel to and outside these lines to delineate the edge of the stencil, creating a border area large enough to show a portion of the motif.

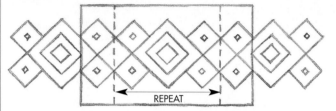

REPEAT

If the design is to be multicolored, color the sketch. Decide how many stencil layers you'll need to accommodate the colors. Colors in areas that are close together should go on separate layers, but if they are somewhat separated, you can probably use one layer to paint more than one color.

### TIPS FROM THE PROS

• Elements that are separated only by a pencil line will merge when cut out of a single stencil layer. Adjacent motifs should be different colors and cut out of separate layers. If you want them to be the same color, add space between them.

• If your design features long slender elements such as tendrils or stems, break them into segments linked by small "bridges." This will make the cut stencil stronger and easier to handle, and the links will hardly be noticeable. If you like, when you've finished stenciling, you can hand-paint these links to fill them in.

Transfer the design to stencil acetate, which is available at art supply stores. Use a fine permanent marker, and for each layer, trace the entire design, being sure to mark the edges of the repeat as well as the outline of the motifs within the border area. Then shade the portions to be cut from that layer. This procedure will mark the repeat and motif alignment on each layer.

Place a marked layer of acetate on a self-healing cutting mat. Use a craft knife to cut out each shaded area. Cut toward yourself and don't lift the knife; when you need to change direction, just rotate the cutting mat while the knife point is down.

### TIPS FROM THE PROS

• If you make a mistake and cut through the edge of a shaded area, you can mend the stencil by applying transparent tape to both sides; recut to remove excess tape.

Each type of paint has its own unique qualities and specific uses. Depending upon the decorative technique you choose, you're likely to need house paint for both the base coat and to make the glaze. For some techniques you'll work with artist's paints, stencil paints, or one or more specialty products. Although paint terminology and the profusion of brand names and grades can be confusing, a basic understanding of paint and related mediums and solvents will help you decide on the right paint for your project.

### PRIMERS

If the surface you intend to paint has never been painted, is porous, or is incompatible with the finish paint, you'll need to prime it. Several types of priming agents are available:

**Primer** Generally used under a flat finish, primer has no sheen. It is available in latex or alkyd format.

**Primer-sealer** For use on new wallboard; this latex primer is usually sold as PVA, or polyvinyl acetate, sealer. (An alkyd primer will raise the nap on the paper covering.)

**Undercoater** This alkyd or latex primer is formulated for use under an enamel finish but can also be used under a flat finish.

### HOUSE PAINTS

The most common types of house paints are water-base (latex) paints and oil-base (alkyd) paints. Their sheens range from flat, or matte, through eggshell and satin to high gloss. There is no industry standard for sheens, so they vary slightly from one manufacturer to another. Before buying paint, decide which decorative technique you will be using. Then purchase the base coat paint with the sheen recommended in the directions for that technique. Glazes can be made with eggshell or satin paint.

**Latex paint** When buying latex paint, choose one containing the greatest quantity of acrylic resin, up to 100%. Vinyl acrylics and other blends are lower in quality. A paint containing solely vinyl resin is the least durable and poorest-quality latex.
• Latex paint dries quickly, usually in a little more than an hour, is practically odorless, and soap and water take care of cleanup. It is not as durable as alkyd paint and tears or turns gummy when sanded.

**Alkyd paint** These oil-base paints, made of synthetic resins, have largely replaced house paints containing linseed and other natural oils. In addition to being less harmful to the environment, they don't smell as much as paints made with natural oils.
• Alkyd paint is durable and stain resistant, dries virtually free of brush marks, and can be sanded easily. It is slow drying and requires paint thinner for cleanup.

### ARTIST'S OILS AND ACRYLICS

Used to tint glazes and for Wood Graining and many other faux finishes, these paints can be found in art supply stores. Both oils and acrylics come in tubes, and acrylics also come in liquid (diluted) form, which is sold in jars. Whatever brand you choose, be consistent if you must buy more of a color before finishing a project. The same color may differ from brand to brand.

### STENCIL PAINTS

Acrylic paints premixed with medium are available in small bottles. Consistency varies among brands, so test before applying to your surface. They can be further mixed with acrylic medium and gel retarder. There is an enormous variety of colors available, some with metallic or pearlized finishes.

### JAPAN COLORS

These quick-drying paints consist of pigments mixed in varnish. They can be used to tint oil-base glazes or for Stenciling if an oil-base finish is desired.

### COMMERCIALLY PREPARED GLAZES

Pretinted water-base glazes, some with metallic or pearlized finishes, can be used wherever a technique calls for a latex wash or an acrylic glaze. Follow the manufacturer's instructions and test to be sure the consistency is appropriate for the effect you wish to achieve.

### SPECIALTY FINISHES

There is a variety of specialty products for crackling, antiquing, and adding a stone, verdigris, or metallic finish. Follow the manufacturer's directions, being sure to use any recommended companion products.

### MAINTAINING A WET EDGE

Throughout this book you'll find references to the *wet edge* and *demarcation lines*. Unless you are painting a very small surface, you will often have to blend two adjacent applications of paint. In order to do this without creating an obvious join (demarcation line), the edge of the first area of paint must almost always be wet when the second area is painted and joined to it (the one exception being between the cut-in and rolled edges of a flat or eggshell latex base coat). And for many decorative techniques the glaze must be wet in order for you to manipulate as well as blend adjacent areas. For this reason you'll find instructions to apply only a specific amount of paint or glaze at one time, along with reminders to work quickly or work with a partner. Conversely, there are times when you must let the paint dry before proceeding. Oil-base glazes stay workable longer than water-base glazes; bear this in mind when choosing paint.

## HOW MUCH PAINT DO YOU NEED?

To figure out how much house paint to buy, you must know the square footage of the area you intend to paint. To determine square footage, measure the width of each wall, add together, then multiply by height. For instance, if a room measures 16 × 20 feet and is 8 feet high, the square footage of the walls is 576 square feet (16 + 16 + 20 + 20 = 72; 72 × 8 = 576). For the ceiling, multiply the width by the length.

Next, estimate how much of the area contains surfaces that won't be painted, such as a fireplace, windows, wallpaper, and areas you'll paint separately, such as woodwork. If those surfaces account for more than 10 percent of the room, deduct the amount from your total. Remember to double your requirement if you're applying two coats. As a rule, the amount of trim—windows, doors, baseboards, and ceiling molding—is proportionate to the amount of wall space by roughly a 1:4 ratio. Therefore, if you're buying 1 gallon of paint for the walls, you'll need a quart for the trim; of course, the number, style, and size of your windows, and whether you are painting the doors as well as the moldings, affect this amount.

Once you know the square footage, refer to the spreading rate printed on the paint can to see approximately how many square feet the can will cover.

Because glazes are thinned, you'll need much less paint to make the glaze for a given area than you'll need for the base coat. In general, you can figure on needing about half the amount of mixed glaze as you would paint, but this depends upon the glaze consistency; refer to the recipes on page 16 and the individual techniques to see the proportions.

### TIPS FROM THE PROS

• 1 gallon of mixed glaze will cover approximately 400 square feet for techniques in which the coverage is dense, such as Sponging Off, Dragging, Rag Rolling, Ragging, Flogging, Stippling, and Combing.

• $^1/_2$ gallon of mixed glaze will cover approximately 400 square feet for techniques in which the coverage is thin, such as Rubbing On or Off, Colorwashing, and Sponging On.

## PREPARING YOUR SURFACE FOR DECORATIVE FINISHES

Before you apply the base coat called for in any decorative technique, you must first be sure your surface is primed appropriately. Following are the most typical surfaces and recommendations for their preparation. In most cases, you'll need to apply two base coats after the primer, lightly sanding between each to ensure proper adhesion of the paint.

| SURFACE | PREPARATION | COMMENTS |
| --- | --- | --- |
| New wallboard | Seal surface with PVA (polyvinyl acetate) sealer; let dry thoroughly. | Don't use alkyd primer—it will raise the nap in the paper. |
| New plaster | Seal surface with vinyl acrylic wall primer; let dry thoroughly. | You can use PVA sealer instead of vinyl acrylic wall primer, but you'll need more to do the same job. |
| Previously painted wallboard or plaster | Treat small stains with white-pigmented shellac, larger ones with quick-drying alkyd primer. Spot-prime patches with PVA sealer or with the base coat paint diluted 10%. If surface is more than 5 years old or there's a big color change, prime entire surface, using vinyl acrylic primer over a latex finish, or alkyd primer over an oil-base finish. | If you're applying an enamel finish over an existing flat finish, prime entire surface to ensure a uniform sheen. |
| Bare wood to be painted | Use alkyd enamel undercoater. (On fir, you can use latex enamel undercoater since fir doesn't bleed.) Let dry overnight. | An enamel finish is usually recommended for wood. |
| Painted wood to be repainted | Chip away loose, flaking paint and sand smooth. Spot-prime bare wood spots with white-pigmented shellac; let dry for 30 minutes. | An enamel finish is usually recommended for wood. |
| Metal | Remove dirt with vinegar. Sand off rust. Prime with rust-inhibitive primer on metal that will rust, latex metal primer on galvanized metal, or conventional metal primer on aluminum. | If applying a specialty finishing product, be sure to follow the manufacturer's recommendations for surface preparation. |

This overview presents some products frequently used to make glazes, lengthen or shorten drying times, or seal finished painting.

## GLAZING LIQUID

The basis for many glazes, glazing liquid is essentially paint without any pigment. Both alkyd and acrylic forms are available in 1-quart and 1-gallon cans.

## ACRYLIC MEDIUM

This is a synthetic resin in transparent gel form used to make water-base glazes. Use a matte, satin, or gloss sheen, not a gel texture.

## PAINT THINNER, MINERAL SPIRITS, TURPENTINE

These volatile liquids are a component of oil-base glazes and are also used for cleanup of alkyd and oil paints. You can use any one of them, but don't switch once you begin a project.

## LINSEED OIL

Pressed oil from the seeds of the flax plant, linseed oil is a component of oil-base glazes, adding sheen and increasing the drying time. For decorative painting, use the quality found in art stores rather than the industrial type found in paint stores.

## JAPAN DRIER

Also called cobalt drier, this chemical speeds drying time for oil-base glazes; it can be found in art and paint stores. The properties of japan drier vary from jar to jar (even in the same brand), some being weaker than others. Only experience can tell you for sure how much to use.

## GEL RETARDER

Also called extender, this is a synthetic substance sometimes mixed with acrylic paint or glaze to retard (slow) its drying time.

## VARNISH

A protective transparent coating, varnish is used to add sheen and extend the life of decorative techniques. It is available in water, oil, and alcohol bases, in finishes ranging from flat to glossy. Varnish is available clear and in a variety of wood stains. Mineral spirit soluble acrylic varnish (MSV) won't yellow light-color oil-painted finishes; it is available at art supply stores.

## SHELLAC

A natural resin, when mixed with alcohol, shellac becomes a fast-drying primer. Available in clear, amber, or white, it can be used over bare or stained wood or as a sealer between coats of oil- and water-base glazes. The descriptor *3- or 5-lb cut* shellac indicates the weight of shellac flakes dissolved in 1 gallon of alcohol. For decorative painting, you sometimes further dilute the shellac.

Most decorative painting techniques are done with glazes or washes. Different painters use the terms *glaze* and *wash* to mean different things. Some people use the term *glaze* only for an oil-base (alkyd) painting medium, and the term *wash* only for a water-base (latex or acrylic) painting medium. In this book *glaze* refers to any thinned paint—either oil or water base—and *wash* refers to a thinned glaze that is translucent or transparent.

## OIL OR WATER BASE?

Many decorative painting techniques can be done using either an oil- or a water-base painting medium—each with its own advantages. The directions for each technique in this book specify the glaze or wash that will be easiest to use for that technique and suggest alternatives whenever appropriate.

Oil glazes, the traditional medium of decorative painters, stay wet and workable longer than water-base glazes and produce a durable and luminous finish. Professionals prefer them for most techniques because they are easier to work with. Mistakes are easy to correct—just dab on paint thinner and wipe off the glaze. Note, however, that handling oil-base paints and thinners requires care because of the chemicals and fumes involved.

• Oil glazes used for large surface decoration are a blend of commercial alkyd glazing liquid, alkyd house paint, and a solvent (paint thinner or mineral spirits).
• Oil glazes used for delicate techniques, such as graining, are a blend of artist's oils, linseed oil, paint thinner, and japan drier.

Latex and acrylic glazes are easy to prepare and clean up—they're mixed and cleaned up with water. However, for some techniques they are more challenging to use than oil-base glazes because they dry relatively quickly. Also, water-base finishes generally don't last as long as oil-base ones, although you can apply a clear coating to protect them. Commercially prepared water-base glazes are specially formulated to stay workable longer.
• Water-base glazes used for large wall decoration are often just a blend of latex house paint and water. The more water, the less intense the color.
• You can alternatively blend commercial acrylic glazing liquid, acrylic paint, water, and acrylic retarder. The glazing liquid extends the glaze without weakening the color.
• Water-base glazes for delicate techniques, such as Wood Graining, are a blend of artist's acrylics, acrylic medium, water, and acrylic retarder. The preceding glazing liquid mixture is also appropriate for delicate techniques when prepared in small quantities.

• The weather affects the drying time of all paints, glazes, and washes. In humid conditions they take longer to dry. In hot weather they dry faster.

## MAKING GLAZES AND WASHES

It is not difficult to mix your own glaze or wash, and doing so gives you great control over the color. Mixing glazes isn't an exact science. In fact, it's more akin to cooking than to chemistry. Don't be afraid to experiment as you become more practiced and confident. Below are some general directions and basic formulas. Look through the book to see the proportions of other glazes and washes. (Glazes for Wood Graining and some other faux finishes are made from artist's paints and mixed on an artist's palette while you work. For more information, see page 17 and the individual techniques.)

## TIPS FROM THE PROS

• Remember, adding glazing liquid extends a glaze, increasing the quantity without affecting the color or thinning the consistency; adding paint thinner or water dilutes both color and consistency.

• Glazes can be opaque or translucent, depending upon the color and the proportions of the ingredients. Some decorative techniques that appear translucent are actually done with opaque glazes—Rubbing is an example.

## Oil Glaze

A good general recipe for beginners, this glaze stays wet even if you work slowly. For faster drying and a harder finish, use less commercial oil glaze and more paint thinner and omit the linseed oil. To mix, pour each ingredient into the paint slowly as you stir.

1 part alkyd paint
1 part alkyd glazing liquid
1 part paint thinner
Small amount of linseed oil (approximately $1/2$ cup per gallon of mixture)

*Best suited for:* Colorwashing, Rubbing, Dragging, Stippling, Ragging, Rag Rolling, Flogging, Combing

## TIPS FROM THE PROS

• Alkyd glazing liquid tends to dry flat. If you want some sheen to your surface, you'll need to add linseed oil. The more oil you add, the shinier your surface will be. Remember that oil is a retarder and increases the drying time of the glaze.

## Latex Glaze or Wash

You can vary this recipe so that water makes up 10–90% of the mixture. The more paint you use, the more durable the finish. The more water, the lighter the color and the more transparent the wash. To mix, pour the water slowly into the paint as you stir.

1 part latex paint
2 parts water

*Best suited for:* Sponging, Limestone, Granite, Colorwashing, Rubbing On

## TIPS FROM THE PROS

• The thinner the latex wash, the weaker (less durable) it is. Professionals say too much water compromises the integrity of a wash. Very thin washes are best used to add tone over another color.

## Acrylic Glaze #1

Mix this glaze in large or small quantities as appropriate.

• For a large quantity, first mix the acrylic paint and glazing liquid until the color is slightly darker than you want (when it's thinned with water, it will lighten up). Gradually add the water until you get the desired consistency.

• For a small quantity, first place the acrylic paint and the glazing liquid separately on an artist's palette. Using a palette knife, spread the paint toward the glazing liquid, mixing to get a color slightly darker than you want. Then transfer the mixture to a container and, while stirring, gradually add the water.

2 parts acrylic paint
1 part acrylic glazing liquid
1 part water
2–4 ounces acrylic gel retarder per gallon (optional)

*Best suited for:* Colorwashing, Spattering, Stamping, Stenciling

## Acrylic Glaze #2

Use this recipe if you don't have access to acrylic glazing liquid.

1 part acrylic paint
1 part acrylic medium (matte, satin, or gloss)
2 parts water (more or less, as desired)
2–4 ounces retarder per gallon (optional)

In general, you'll find it easier and have more consistent results if you use house paints to color glazes for walls and other large surfaces. There are thousands of custom color chips to choose from. Many paint stores can even use a computer to scan a color sample, such as a fabric swatch, and then tint paint to match it. For techniques involving hand-painting with artist's or stencil paints, you can mix colors as necessary or desired.

## TINTING COLORS

Should you wish to alter a paint color yourself, remember that japan colors or artist's oils are compatible with oil glazes, and artist's acrylics are compatible with water-base glazes. You can also use universal tints to color any medium. However, never tint more than the percentage recommended by the manufacturer on the bottle or tube of universal tint, or your glaze won't dry. Keep in mind that latex paint is much darker when dry than while wet, so you'll have to experiment until you get the color you desire.

## TIPS FROM THE PROS

• Because of the experimentation required and difficulty of duplicating the results, you're likely to find that tinting your own glazes is costly, time-consuming, and frustrating. Reserve tinting for techniques such as Wood Graining or Stenciling, which don't use large amounts of color.
• Universal tints are pure pigment. They contain none of the binders that make paint. That's why you can use them with either medium and why too much of them keeps the paint from drying.

## DILUTING COLORS

You may want to have various values of a color, for instance, when painting Limestone, in which all the glaze colors should be closely related, or when creating an ombré effect, in which graduated colors blend seamlessly. To achieve three different values of the same color, purchase house paint in the darkest value. Pour half into another container and add enough white or off-white paint to lighten it to half the original intensity. Then pour half of that paint into a third container and mix again with white to produce the lightest value. Then, following the appropriate recipe, mix a glaze using each value.

## USING THE ARTIST'S PALETTE

For faux finishes such as Marble or Wood Graining, instead of working with a liquid glaze, you'll use small amounts of artist's oils or acrylics, mixing them with a medium as you work. Following the specific technique directions, mix the medium (see page 18) and squeeze a small dab of each artist's color onto an artist's palette.

**1** Dip the brush into the medium and then into the specified colors, picking up a small amount of each.

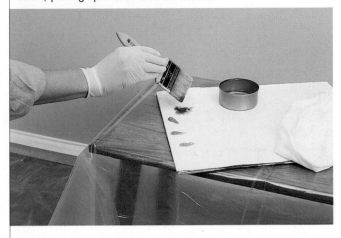

**2** Then, as directed, either mix the colors by swirling your brush on the palette or apply them to your surface without mixing. The latter method allows for more variation in the color, which looks realistic in some faux techniques. With experience you'll learn to adjust the amount of medium required for each step.

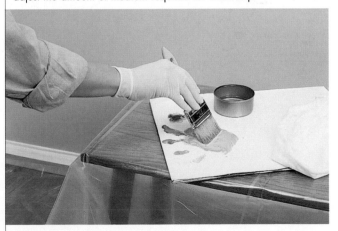

## TIPS FROM THE PROS

• Pour the medium into a small container, such as a clean, empty tuna can, and tape it onto your palette.
• Place the palette on a nearby worktable or on the floor so you don't have to hold it while you're painting.

• If you're doing a large Wood Graining project—for instance, several doors—you might want to premix a batch of the colors before you start. While you won't get the subtle variations of the previous technique, you will be assured of getting consistent colors. Store the mixed colors in sealed plastic food containers or jars.

• To keep premixed oil colors from drying out, pour some linseed oil on top and seal the containers. When you're ready to paint, carefully pour off the linseed oil into another container. At the end of the painting session, pour the linseed oil back into each container. (You can pour the oil from different colors into the same container.)

**Oil mediums** The medium for artist's oils is a mixture of linseed oil and thinner mixed with a little japan drier to speed the drying time. There are two recipes, one containing a greater proportion of oil. The technique directions specify which to use with each step. You can mix the linseed oil and thinner ahead of time, label it with the recipe number, and store it indefinitely in a glass jar, but don't add the japan drier until instructed.

**TIPS FROM THE PROS**

• A little medium goes a long way (1 cup is sufficient for graining four doors). If you are painting a small area, read the technique directions before you mix the medium to see how much should be placed in the container, then measure the tablespoon quantity of each ingredient and add the drier as indicated. This amount will probably be enough to get you through the first phase of your project.

**Oil Medium #1**

1 part linseed oil
2 parts thinner
Japan drier (added later)

**Oil Medium #2**

1 part oil
1 part thinner
Japan drier (added later)

**Acrylic medium** The medium for artist's acrylics is a blend of acrylic medium and gel retarder; water is added for use with tube acrylics. Mix the medium in a small container, seal, and label. You can store it indefinitely. If you are using liquid acrylics, you can just pour a small amount of straight acrylic medium and retarder onto your palette and blend them into the paints as you work.

**Acrylic Medium**

1 part acrylic medium (matte, satin, or gloss)
2 parts water (more or less as desired)
Retarder (no more than 15% of the total mixture)

## SAFETY PRECAUTIONS

Exercise caution when working with paint. Following are some basic safety guidelines.

• Carefully read the labels on cans of paint and related mediums for warnings about possible hazards and heed all safety instructions.

• If you are using paper towels or rags to work with or to clean up oil or alkyd paint, paint thinner, or any other flammable liquid, submerge them in a bucket of water as soon as they are no longer usable. When your project is finished, spread out the rags to dry outdoors or in a well-ventilated room and do not leave them unattended overnight. Dispose of them according to local ordinances.

**TIPS FROM THE PROS**

• Every professional painter can recount a terrible tale of spontaneous combustion. NEVER fold or wad oil-soaked rags or paper towels and then set them aside or throw them into a trash can or bag.

• Never smoke while painting or while using thinner. Don't use a hair dryer to speed the drying of thinner-cleaned brushes.

• Wear an approved respirator, a type of mask that will filter vapors. Respirators are available at paint and hardware stores.

• Always work with paint products in a well-ventilated area. Open doors and windows and use exhaust fans. Excessive inhalation of fumes from paints and solvents can cause dizziness, headaches, fatigue, and nausea.

• Wear a dust mask when you're sanding.

• Wear latex gloves to protect your hands from solvents.

• Wear safety goggles when painting overhead.

• Keep paint and paint products out of the reach of children. Keep pets and young children out of freshly painted rooms; paint fumes are especially harmful to pet birds.

• Inspect ladders for sturdiness. Make sure all four legs are resting squarely on the floor and both cross braces are locked in place. Never stand on the top step or the utility shelf. Never lean away from a ladder; instead, get off and move it if you can't reach a spot easily.

# PAINTING BASICS

Everyone, at one time or another, has done some painting. But while the act of painting itself requires no special knack, a knowledge of basic procedures makes the job easier and ensures pleasing results. Whether you're applying a base coat or painting a decorative finish, many of the basic processes are the same. For a successful job it's essential to know what tools to use, what type of paint to choose, the sequence in which to work, and the technique for applying the paint or glaze.

## GETTING READY

Decide first which decorative technique you will be using, then determine what kind of paint to buy: latex or alkyd; eggshell, satin, or semigloss. If you are painting a new surface, prime it before applying the base coat, being sure to use the appropriate type of primer. For more information on paint, see pages 13–14.

Before you begin to paint, gather any equipment you'll need (see pages 8–9). The directions in this book begin with a list of the tools and materials essential to each technique but do not include ladders, drop cloths, or protective clothing other than gloves. Also determine the painting sequence (below) and then protect the floor and any furniture with drop cloths.

## PAINTING SEQUENCE

The best way to avoid painting yourself into a corner, spattering paint onto newly painted surfaces, or inadvertently touching a just-painted edge is to follow a painting sequence. First paint the ceiling—if you'll be giving it a decorative treatment, do so before proceeding to the walls. Then paint the base coat onto the walls and apply your chosen decorative finish. Finally, paint the woodwork, beginning at the ceiling—first any crown molding and then the windows, doors, cabinets, and baseboards.

**Decorative techniques** When applying a decorative finish, you must consider the best order in which to paint each surface—from right to left or left to right and in consecutive or alternate components.

• Whether you begin at the right or left edge is almost always up to you. Generally, right-handed people will be more comfortable working from left to right; left-handed, from right to left. The important thing is that you not smear your work as you progress.

• In general, you paint alternate or nonadjacent components so the paint on each can dry and then be protected while you paint the adjacent section. If you are painting an entire room, complete opposite walls first, then complete the alternate walls. Be sure the paint on the first walls is dry before masking them in the corners.

• For most decorative techniques you should work from top to bottom. This minimizes damage to the painted area from inadvertent spatters or a dropped brush. Refer to the specific techniques for more information. Refer to pages 28–29 for painting door and window components.

### TIPS FROM THE PROS

• Most of the step-by-step photographs in this book show a right-handed painter working from right to left. This was done so the painter's body wouldn't block the camera's view of the painted surface. You should do what is most comfortable.

• Some processes can be done with the tools in either hand. If the painter in the photo is holding a tool in her left hand, it is because she found it comfortable to do so. Using both hands prevents fatigue during a large project.

**Woodwork** If you're giving new woodwork a stain or clear finish, do so before painting the walls. If you're painting new or previously painted woodwork, lightly sand the surface so the new paint will adhere. Make sure your walls and woodwork are clean and free of dust.

### TIPS FROM THE PROS

• To achieve a smooth surface for decorative painting, professionals often brush over the paint after it's been rolled on. This is easier to do with alkyd paint; latex dries too quickly.

• For best adherence, apply all coats of paint within about two weeks of each other.

## PAINTING A SAMPLE

Most of the techniques presented in this book take practice to master. You can paint a sample on paper or directly on the wall.

**Sampling on paper** Use a piece of bristol board, a thick paper that can be purchased in an art supply store, or tag board, an inexpensive stiff paper available in most art or stationery stores. Use a piece at least 15" × 20" so you'll be able to get a feel for the process and judge the effect of the finished painting. Prime the board first with oil-base primer so that it won't bubble or buckle. Then apply two layers of the base coat before you begin experimenting with the glaze. When the test is done, tape it on the wall with low-tack tape (after the base coat on the wall is dry) so you can see the effect in the room in various light conditions.

### TIPS FROM THE PROS

• Professionals tape one end of each sample board to a wire coat hanger. They hang the wet boards on a coat rack to dry. If you are making a number of samples, try this—it will save space and prevent anyone from walking on work placed on the floor.

**Sampling on a wall** Professionals often test a technique directly on the wall or other surface they plan to paint. To do this, apply the base coat and let it dry, then mask out an area approximately 15" × 20" with brown paper painter's tape. Apply the glaze and manipulate it in whatever method you've chosen. If you need to continue to practice or if you change your mind on the particular technique, wipe off the glaze and start again. Once you're satisfied with the effect, wipe off the glaze completely with a rag saturated with paint thinner or water, as appropriate. The tape will prevent the glaze from smearing into a larger area. This test is easy to do if you are using an oil-base glaze, but a fast-drying water-base glaze will be difficult to remove.

## TIPS FROM THE PROS

• To see the effect of a technique in different light, let the sample dry. Observe it at different times of day. Then paint it out with your base coat paint. Though this adds a day or two to your project, it saves time and money in the long run.

## STANDING BACK AS YOU PAINT

It's easy to get caught up in your work as you develop a rhythm of applying the paint or manipulating the glaze. But it's important to put down your roller, brush, or other applicator occasionally and stand back to see the overall effect. When you're standing close to your work, it's difficult to get any real perspective.

If you do this early on, you'll be able to make any necessary adjustments to get the effect you desire. As you continue to work, you'll want to ensure that you're applying the paint or manipulating the glaze in a consistent manner.

## MASKING

Unless you have an extremely steady hand, it's a good idea to protect surfaces immediately adjacent to where you'll be painting by covering them with masking tape. Be sure to use the right masking tape for the job. Generally, 3" brown paper painter's tape, which has one sticky edge, is suitable. Blue low-tack tape is good for delicate painted surfaces, but it's expensive. You can also buy pre-taped plastic drop cloths, which can be used to cover larger areas, and painter's plastic, which adheres with static electricity and is good for protecting woodwork or wallpaper. To mask narrow faux grout or inlay lines, see Stripes and Grids, page 84.

Always remove masking tape promptly so that the adhesive doesn't damage the walls or leave a residue. Don't leave tape on overnight, even if you plan to apply a second coat of paint the next day. Instead, apply new tape for each painting session.

## BROWN PAPER PAINTER'S TAPE

**1** Apply the tape with the sticky edge adjacent to the area you'll be painting.

## TIPS FROM THE PROS

• To ensure a tight seal, you can run a putty knife along the tape.
• If you are masking a large area, use an automatic tape dispenser to speed up the job.

**2** To remove tape, unpeel one end, fold it back so that it is approximately parallel to the painted surface, and gently pull. Change your grip as needed.

## TIPS FROM THE PROS

• If you hold the tape perpendicular to the painted surface while you pull, you're more likely to pull off paint along with the tape.
• If you have difficulty removing the tape, try loosening it by warming it with a hair dryer.

## PRE-TAPED PLASTIC DROP CLOTH

Available in rolls, this is a sheet of folded plastic with masking tape along one edge. It's very useful for protecting large or convoluted surfaces, especially if you are spattering.

**1** Apply the folded plastic with the tape edge adjacent to the area you'll be painting.

**2** Unfold the plastic. Static electricity will hold the plastic against the surface.

**3** To remove the tape, unpeel one end, fold it back so that it is approximately parallel to the painted surface, and gently pull. Change your grip as needed and be careful not to mar wet paint with the plastic.

There is a right way to do even this seemingly obvious part of the painting process.

### LOADING A BRUSH

Before loading your brush for the first time, roll the bristles between your palms to remove any loose bristles. Then shake the brush vigorously.

**With paint or glaze** Hold the brush vertically and dip it into the paint or glaze, covering half the length of the bristles. Dip 2–4 times to thoroughly saturate the bristles. If this is the first time you're loading the brush, gently stir the paint or glaze with it so that the bristles spread slightly; don't stir when reloading.

Lift the brush straight up and let the excess paint or glaze drip into the bucket. Gently slap both sides of the brush against the inside of the bucket 2–3 times. Do not wipe the edges of the brush against the lip of the bucket or the bristles may clump and, if you are painting from a resealable container, the seal will not be tight.

## LOADING A ROLLER

Before using a new napped roller, you should remove the excess lint from it. Unroll a length of 3" masking tape (regular, not painter's), hold the end in one hand, and place the roll between your knees or feet. Place the roller sleeve on a roller frame and roll it back and forth over the tape. This is not necessary if you're using a foam roller.

**With paint** If you're working with paint, pour 1–2 gallons into a 5-gallon bucket fixed with a wire mesh grid. Dip the roller into the paint and roll it over the grid a couple of times to spread the paint evenly and squeeze out the excess.

**With glaze** If you're working with glaze, pour some into the well of a paint tray. Dip the roller into the glaze and roll it over the slanted surface of the tray until it becomes saturated with glaze. Using the inside crescent of the curved painter's tool, scrape off the excess glaze all around the roller.

Tap the end of the roller onto a folded paper towel to blot any remaining glaze.

There are two basic steps to applying either a base coat of paint or a glaze that will be removed to create a decorative effect: cutting in—painting a border along the edges of your surface—and rolling on—filling in the surface with a roller loaded with paint. Depending upon the paint type or the decorative technique, you may work on an entire wall or only a portion at one time.

When applying primer or base coat, use a roller wherever you can—rolling on paint is much easier and faster than brushing it on. Use a brush to cut in areas that will be rolled and also to paint woodwork. When using a brush, never work directly from the paint can. Instead, stir the paint, pour it into a bucket, and stir it again. If your job requires two or more cans of paint, pour an equal amount of paint from each can into your bucket and mix to eliminate any slight color variations. If you are painting a small area, you can use a roller tray instead of a bucket.

## PREPARING THE SURFACE

Before applying the first coat of primer or paint, or between coats of dry paint or glaze, smooth out any imperfections by going over the surface with superfine sandpaper wrapped around a block—being sure to sand walls as well as woodwork. Be on the lookout for dried paint drips or any raised seams created by drywall tape. After sanding, brush off the dust with a clean soft brush and remove residue with a tack cloth.

## TIPS FROM THE PROS
• Use a vacuum cleaner after extensive sanding.

## CUTTING IN

It is difficult to apply paint or glaze neatly in a corner or along molding with a roller, so before you begin to paint a wall or ceiling, you should cut in the edges with a paintbrush—a 2"–3" trim brush is ideal (a foam brush is ideal for glaze). To cut in, first mask with tape the edges of moldings or any fixtures that cannot be removed. If the wall and ceiling (or adjacent walls) will be different colors, you can mask the edge of whichever you are not painting or use an edge guide to keep paint from straying onto the adjacent surface. Paint along all the perimeter edges, as well as along the fixtures. For decorative painting, be sure to follow the directions for cutting in given with each technique.

## TIPS FROM THE PROS
• If you're using flat or eggshell latex paint, you can cut in the entire room before rolling on a base coat of paint.
• If you're using latex enamel or any alkyd, you'll get better results cutting in a small section and then filling it in with a roller before moving on to the next section. Do not let the edge of one section dry before starting another, or you will get a demarcation line. For best results when painting a base coat, work with a partner, one of you cutting in the edges, one rolling on the paint.

**1** Dip the trim brush in paint, position it on the edge of the wall or ceiling about two brush lengths from a corner, and paint toward the corner using long, overlapping strokes.

**2** Repeat, starting about two brush lengths from where you began before. Blend the paint into the wet edge.

**3** Continue in this manner until you reach the next corner.
• For a ceiling, repeat along each edge as appropriate and then cut in any hanging fixtures.
• For a wall, cut in first along the ceiling, then above the baseboard, next around door and window frames, then around any lighting fixtures, and finally along the vertical corners.

## ROLLING ON PAINT

The overall process for rolling on paint is the same whether you're painting a ceiling or wall. The object is to create a covering that appears seamless. To do this, roll the paint onto a fairly small area in a zigzag pattern and then, without lifting the roller, roll over the same area in different directions to spread the paint. If you are painting a ceiling or a high wall, you'll probably find it easier to work if you first fit an extension handle onto your roller handle.

**TIPS FROM THE PROS**

• To minimize spattering, be sure to roll the excess paint off your roller every time you load it.

**1** Load your roller with paint and off-load the excess. Roll on the paint in a large zigzig pattern to cover an area about 3' × 4'. Roll diagonally upward first and keep the roller against the surface as you change direction. Keep a light, even pressure on the roller.

**2** Without reloading or lifting the roller, roll back diagonally across the first zigzag, filling in unpainted areas.

**3** Still without reloading or lifting the roller, roll back over the same area, applying more pressure to the roller and keeping it nearly parallel to the 4' edge (here the vertical edge).

**TIPS FROM THE PROS**

• On the final length, gradually decrease the pressure on the roller. Then avoid spinning it as you lift it off the painted surface.
• It really doesn't matter whether you first roll toward or away from the corner. Just be sure to make opposing zigzags followed by a straight path.

**4** Repeat below or next to the completed section.

**TIPS FROM THE PROS**

• When painting a wall, start at a top corner (left if you're right-handed; right if you're left-handed) for the first section. Make the next zigzag below the first section.
• When painting a ceiling, always work perpendicular to the longer edge and go all the way across the narrower dimension in 4' lengths.

**5** When you have completed one length (top to bottom for a wall; an entire width for a ceiling), roll the unloaded roller in one long straight stroke along the leading edge (the edge adjacent to the unpainted area).

## ROLLING ON GLAZE

When you roll on glaze, you want it to cover the surface evenly and without drips but still be wet enough to manipulate. Because glaze is thinner than paint, it tends to run when you apply it, and you may have to roll over it several times to get the proper coverage.

**1** Load your roller with glaze and scrape off the excess with the curved painter's tool.

**2** Starting at the top and working down to the baseboard, roll on one roller width of glaze. Repeat as indicated in the technique directions.

**3** Without reloading the roller, reroll the applied glaze until the coverage is uniform.

### TIPS FROM THE PROS

• You can roll on the glaze from top to bottom and then reroll with a narrow zigzag path, or do the reverse.
• You can also brush out the applied glaze with a house painter's or chip brush. Brush back and forth in all directions.

Only with experience will you be able to tell when the glaze is behaving properly. Here are a few pointers.
• If you are painting a small area, you may have to wait a few minutes for the glaze to set before you start to manipulate it.
• If you apply too much glaze—which can happen if you don't scrape enough off the roller or if you misjudge the size of the area—roll it out, wipe off some with a rag, and then reroll. Or use a clean roller to roll off some of the excess.
• If the glaze is too thin, wipe it off and reformulate the mixture by adding more paint; if the glaze color changes, add proportionately less glazing liquid (and linseed oil, if applicable) than in the original mixture.

## TEAMWORK

Although a few decorative paint effects are created by applying glaze to a small portion of a surface with a brush, rag, or sponge, most effects involve covering a relatively large portion of the surface with glaze and then removing some of it. To do this, you have to work quickly so that you can seamlessly blend one section into the previous one before the glaze dries. You'll find it much easier to do this if you work with a partner. One of you can apply the glaze and the other can manipulate it. To avoid getting in each other's way, follow these steps.

**1** The first person should begin at a top corner and roll a strip of glaze between the ceiling and the baseboard as indicated in the specific technique directions.

**2** The second person should begin to manipulate the applied glaze. At the same time, the first person should roll another strip adjacent to the first, overlapping the wet edge slightly.

**3** Continue in this manner until the entire wall is completed.

### TIPS FROM THE PROS

• To work together successfully, each partner must be sensitive to what the other is doing. Depending upon the technique and the height of the wall, the person rolling on the glaze may need to take small breaks so as not to get too far ahead.
• If you are the roller, you'll also be responsible for cutting in the glaze as necessary.

# HANDLING CORNERS

Corners are one of the trickier aspects of decorative painting. Glaze tends to gather and build up in corners, which can detract from the overall appearance of the finish. The following processes are specific to individual techniques, but if you understand them all, you'll be able to adapt them to various situations. And should you make an error while working, one of the following may offer a quick fix.

## COLORWASHING

Do not cut in the corner. Lay on the glaze, stopping several inches from the adjacent wall. With the same brush, work the glaze into and then away from the corner. If needed, you can use a dry brush to pull out any buildup of paint.

## RAGGING

Cut the glaze into the corner. Rag the area of wall near the corner as explained in the directions. Bunch up the rag as necessary so that it fits into the corner.

## RAG ROLLING

Cut in the corner. Roll on the glaze. Roll the rag cylinder from ceiling to baseboard. Then use the end of the cylinder or another, smaller cylinder to blot any missed areas.

## RUBBING OFF

You can cut in the corners, but if you are unsure of your skill or speed, work as follows: Do not cut in the corner. Brush or roll on a small section of glaze, starting 1"–2" from the adjacent wall. Rub the glaze into the corner with a rag. Pounce a clean brush (tap the bristle tips) into the corner to fill in any missing spots. Then continue to rub the applied glaze.

## HORIZONTAL CORNERS

Handle the join between a wall and ceiling, crown molding, floor, or baseboard the same way you do a vertical corner.

## RUBBING ON

You can cut in the corners, but if you are unsure of your skill or speed, work as follows: Don't cut in the corner. Instead, rub on some glaze close to the corner, then use a chip brush to dab the rubbed glaze into the corner and another chip brush to pounce it out. Use the brushes alternately, switching from one to the other as needed. Then continue to rub the applied glaze.

## STIPPLING

You can cut in the corners, but if you are unsure of your skill or speed, work as follows: Do not cut in the corner. Roll on the glaze, starting $1/2"$ from the adjacent wall. Pounce the glaze into the corner with a chip brush, then change to the stippling brush and work the rest of the glaze. You have to work very quickly when stippling.

## SPONGING OFF

Cut in the corner. Roll on the glaze. Tear off a small piece of sponge. While you are working with the large sponge, intermittently dab the small piece into the corner to continue the pattern on any remaining small areas of glaze. Work with one sponge in each hand if you find it comfortable.

## SPONGING ON

Do not cut in the corner. Tear off a small piece of sponge. Load it with glaze and dab it into the corner. You can fill in the corners as you go or do them all at once at the end.

## PAINTING MOLDINGS

You'll probably need two or three paintbrushes to apply a primer or the base coat to moldings: a narrow angled sash brush for return edges or relief areas and one or two wider flat brushes for the molding face. If possible, use a brush the same width as the section to be painted. Professionals don't mask the adjacent wall edges because the tape is difficult to apply with a good seal and makes it difficult to see what they're doing, but you can mask if you wish. Cut in edges or returns and then paint the remaining portion, switching brushes as appropriate.

Follow the specific technique directions to apply a decorative finish to molding. Bear in mind that sponged techniques are difficult to apply to relief surfaces.

**1** Begin about 3" from a corner (or end) and brush the paint toward the corner. Reverse direction and, brushing over the applied paint, brush away from the corner. This will help spread the paint evenly. If the paint is still wet, brush lightly over the painted area again to obscure any brush strokes.

**2** Repeat, beginning a few inches from where you stopped and brushing the paint first into the wet edge and then in the opposite direction.

**3** When you reach the opposite corner, brush into the corner and then out.

### TIPS FROM THE PROS

• Always brush in the direction of the wood grain, parallel to the long edge of the molding. Follow the joints of the woodwork to change direction.

• To protect carpeting, use a drop cloth and a flexible edge guide.

• To mask flooring, first apply painter's tape adjacent to the baseboard, then tape a drop cloth over the tape, leaving a 1" painter's tape border.

### PAINTING WINDOWS

If you wish, mask the walls adjacent to the window frame. Also tape the edges of the glass so you don't scratch it later by scraping off paint. If possible, remove any locking hardware or mask it with tape. Whether you're painting a double-hung or casement window, paint the sash first, then the molding.

Lightly load an angled sash brush with paint. As you brush on the paint, let it slightly overlap the tape so that the paint seeps into the crevice between the glass and wood. This will seal the finish to the glass, so that any condensation forming on the glass won't get under the paint and cause peeling.

**Double-hung windows** If the sashes are removable, lift them out, lay them on a table, and paint them. Be prepared to leave the sashes out long enough to dry thoroughly. If the sashes aren't removable, you'll need to raise and lower them as needed to reach all parts of the window.

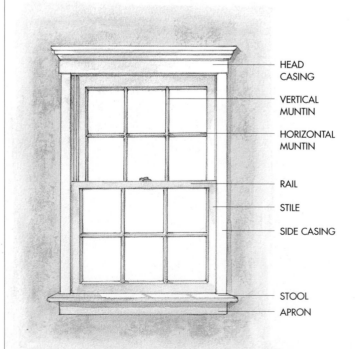

HEAD CASING

VERTICAL MUNTIN

HORIZONTAL MUNTIN

RAIL

STILE

SIDE CASING

STOOL

APRON

Paint the outer, or upper, sash first. If the window has small panes, begin with the horizontal muntins and then work on the vertical ones. Then paint the exposed parts of the stiles, the top rail, and the bottom rail, in that order. Do not paint the bottom underside of the sash, which should be painted with exterior paint. Paint the inner, or lower, sash in the same manner, finishing by painting the top of the sash.

## TIPS FROM THE PROS

• To prevent nonremovable sashes from sticking, be sure to leave each slightly raised or lowered so that you'll be able to move it once or twice while the paint is drying.

**Casement windows** First, paint any vertical muntins and then any horizontal ones. Next, paint the top rails, bottom rails, and stiles. Finally, paint the casing.

**Window molding** To paint the trim around a double-hung window, begin with the head casing, then paint down the sides. Next, paint the stool and then finish with the apron. Promptly remove masking tape.

## PAINTING DOORS

Remove any hardware from the door. If that's not possible, mask the hardware with tape. Always paint a door from the top to the bottom. Paint the vertical edges to match the face of the door that is exposed when the door is open; do not paint the top or bottom edges.

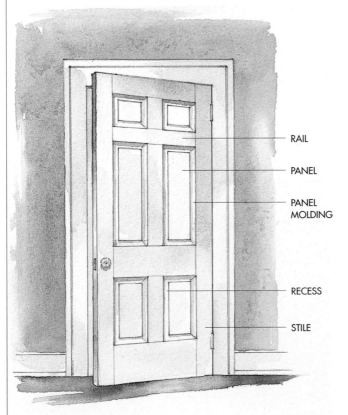

RAIL

PANEL

PANEL MOLDING

RECESS

STILE

**For a solid color** When painting a panel door a solid color, work in the following order: panel moldings, recesses, panels, rails, and stiles. Always brush in the direction of the wood grain.

## TIPS FROM THE PROS

• To paint flat doors, roll on the paint and then brush it out smoothly in the direction of the wood grain.

**For a faux finish** When painting a panel door with a faux finish, you should generally work from top to bottom and left to right (right to left if you are left-handed), completing all stiles and panels before painting the rails. This will minimize the chances of accidentally marring completed portions as you work. However, because the drying time and painting complexity vary with the technique, you'll have to use some judgment. Determine the appropriate way to paint the panel moldings and recesses before you begin; usually they can be worked from left to right as part of the panel painting, but this may depend upon the technique and the molding details.

## TIPS FROM THE PROS

• For most faux finishing techniques, each door component must dry before the adjacent one can be painted. Allow plenty of time.

**Door molding** To paint the trim around a door, begin with the head casing, then paint down the sides. If the door opens away from the room, paint the jamb and the two surfaces of the door stop. If the door opens into the room, paint the jamb and the door side of the door stop.

Do not close the door until all the paint is thoroughly dry.

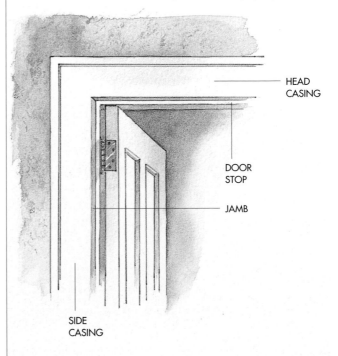

HEAD CASING

DOOR STOP

JAMB

SIDE CASING

# HOLDING BRUSHES

Successful brushwork relies as much on technique as on talent. You'll be off to a good start if you hold the brush correctly for each specific process. This photograph shows the basic anatomy of a brush.

BRISTLES

FERRULE

2½"
63.5 mm

HANDLE

## FLOGGING AND DRAGGING

Grasp the paintbrush handle in your fist and brace your thumb against the ferrule. When you work, hold the brush so that the bristles point in the direction you'll flog or the handle points in the direction you'll drag.

## DETAILING

For lining, hold a script liner or touch-up brush tightly at the ferrule, as if holding a pen; raise your pinkie and place it against the surface being painted to steady your hand.

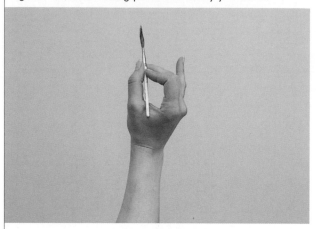

For veining, hold a script liner firmly midway down the handle between your forefinger, middle finger, and thumb; keep your wrist flexible.

## CREATING UNDULATIONS

Grasp a house painter's brush firmly at the ferrule, extending your fingers onto the bristles. When you work, place the bristles at a 45° angle to the surface.

## SOFTENING

Hold the paintbrush between your thumb and four fingers at the ferrule. Keep your wrist flexible. When you work, touch just the tips of the bristles to the surface and whisk them back and forth very lightly.

### TIPS FROM THE PROS

• Hold a paintbrush this way for regular painting too, but apply more pressure when you work. This grip gives you good control and flexibility and is less tiring than holding the brush by the handle.

### SPATTERING

Grasp the paintbrush handle in your fist and hold the brush with the bristles up and the narrow face toward the wall. Place the handle of the spatter stick in front of and perpendicular to the paintbrush and pull the stick toward you across the bristle tips. It doesn't matter which hand you use to hold each tool, and you can switch them from hand to hand as you work.

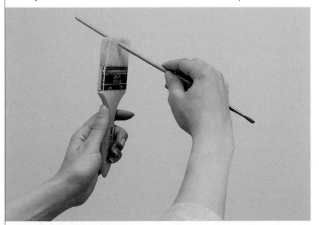

## STENCILING

Grasp the brush at the ferrule between your forefinger, middle finger, and thumb; position it perpendicular to the surface.

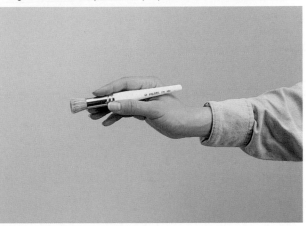

## VEINING

Hold a fan brush, short-bristled artist's brush, or veiner near the tip of the handle between your forefinger, middle finger, and thumb; keep your grasp loose and flexible.

Sealing decorative painting with varnish or wax is optional for some techniques and integral to others, particularly the faux finishes. Sealers add sheen and protect the painting, making it more durable and easier to clean. Woodwork, floors, and furniture can be sealed by anyone, but it is extremely difficult to varnish walls and this should be left to professionals.

Varnishes are formulated with an alkyd or water base. For best results, use alkyd-base varnishes over all faux finishes—whether oil or water base. Should you decide to have your walls varnished, request a water-base varnish, regardless of the glaze formulation. Many varnishes come in a full range of sheens: flat, eggshell, satin, semigloss, gloss, and high gloss. When choosing a sheen, consider the final effect you'd like—some faux finishes such as granite and marble can be either matte or glossy, depending on whether you're imitating a honed or polished surface. Polyurethane, which also comes in alkyd and water base, can be used instead of varnish but is not appropriate for sealing any work done with artist's oils.

For best protection, apply two or three coats of varnish. Dilute the first coat, using 8 parts varnish to 2 parts mineral spirits (for an alkyd varnish) or water (for a water-base varnish). If applying three coats, use 9 parts varnish diluted with 1 part mineral spirits or water. The final coat should be full strength in either case.

Before varnishing, make sure your surface is completely dry and dust free. Brush on the varnish using a brush specifically set aside for the task. Polyurethane can be applied to large surfaces with a mohair or foam roller. Let dry. Between coats, lightly sand the varnish using 600- or 800-grit wet or dry sandpaper, and then wipe the surface with a tack cloth.

In place of varnish, you can use white refined beeswax, which does not yellow and is ideal for light-colored finishes, especially white faux marble. Rub the wax on the surface using a cotton or linen cloth. Let it set, then buff with a clean cloth.

### TIPS FROM THE PROS
• You can wax a varnished surface, but you cannot top a waxed surface with varnish or polyurethane.

Immediately after you've finished using your tools, clean them. If you've used latex paint, all you'll need is soap and water to clean up. Tools used with alkyd paints or artist's oils must be cleaned with paint thinner. Always let tools dry completely before storing them.

It's not necessary to clean brushes and rollers if you plan to return to your project shortly. Brushes will keep for a few days if you hang them in the appropriate solvent. Alternatively, you can wrap brushes in foil or plastic and put those used with alkyd paint in the freezer and those used with latex in the refrigerator. Rollers or applicator pads will keep overnight in a plastic bag in the refrigerator.

### TIPS FROM THE PROS
• To remove a roller sleeve for short-term storage, slide it back into its orginal wrapper, grasp firmly, and pull out the roller frame.

• If you're stopping just for lunch, leave the bagged sleeve on the frame and hang or prop it in the paint bucket or tray (be sure not to submerge it in the paint).

### CLEANING BRUSHES
Make sure you've eliminated as much paint from the brush as possible before cleaning it. You can brush it on cardboard, paper towels, or newsprint. Brushes used with washes and glazes are usually easier to clean than those used with thicker house paints.

**Latex paint** Hold the brush under running water until the water runs clear. Then wash the brush with soap and lukewarm water, forcing water into the bristles at the ferrule. Rinse well and blot on paper towels.

**Alkyd paint** Dip the bristles into a container of paint thinner and work the brush against the sides and bottom. If necessary, work thinner into the bristles with your hands, especially near the ferrule. Blot the brush on paper towels.

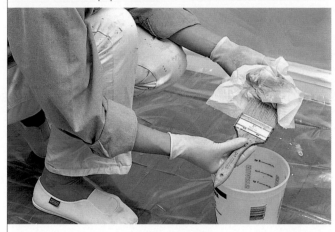

When the brush is clean, remove the excess thinner by wiping the bristles on paper towels. Then wash the brush in warm water with yellow or white bar soap and blot again.

### TIPS FROM THE PROS

• Use several containers of thinner, removing most of the paint in the first, more in the second, and so on.

• If a brush is unusually saturated, after you've removed as much paint as possible with the appropriate solvent, run a wire comb through the bristles to remove more paint. Rinse the brush in water or thinner again.

• Paint and hardware stores sell a special spinning clamp designed to expel liquid from brushes. These brush spinners are handy; use them lowered into a large bucket or, to spin off water, outdoors.

### CLEANING ROLLERS

You may find it's easier to dispose of rollers than to clean them, especially since they're relatively inexpensive. Those with cardboard tubes don't survive the cleaning well anyway.

Place the roller in a paint bucket with a rack or in a paint tray and scrape off the excess paint with a curved painter's tool.

Roll the roller back and forth over the rack or tray. Then remove the roller cover.

**Latex paint** Hold the roller under running water until the water runs clear. Wash the roller with dish detergent and lukewarm water, forcing water into the nap. Rinse, squeeze out the excess water, and blot lightly with paper towels. Wash the roller frame handle with soap and water.

**Alkyd paint** Wash the roller in a container of paint thinner, forcing thinner into the nap. When clean, squeeze out the excess thinner and blot on paper towels. Then wash with warm water and dish detergent and blot again. Clean the roller frame handle with thinner.

### TIPS FROM THE PROS

• Place roller covers on end to allow any water or paint thinner to drain and to prevent the nap from flattening.

### CLEANING CONTAINERS

Transfer leftover paint or glaze to a storage container. Wipe out reusable buckets, mixing containers, and roller trays with paper towels. Use thinner or detergent and water to clean them, as appropriate.

## CLEANING YOURSELF

Wet or dry latex paint readily washes off skin. Latex that has dried doesn't wash off clothing, however, so be sure to launder your painting clothes before the paint has dried completely.

If you've used alkyd paint, your best bet is a mechanic's hand cleaner. It's easier on your skin than paint thinner and just as effective. Also use the hand cleaner to get fresh alkyd paint out of your clothing, then launder the clothes immediately.

## STORING CLEANED EQUIPMENT

When dry, wrap brushes in the original or a homemade stiff paper cover. Store them flat or hanging. Store roller covers in sealed plastic bags.

## STORING LEFTOVER PAINT

Most leftover paint can be stored in a tightly closed container for several months or more. If less than a quarter of the paint in a can remains, transfer it to a container small enough to be almost filled. Less air in the can means the paint is less likely to dry out.

If you are storing paint or mixed glazes in a can, wipe any paint from the rim. Cover the can with the lid and tap it firmly with a hammer to seal.

If you are storing mixed glazes, be sure to label the containers—especially if you've used several related glazes or have several strengths of one hue. Indicate whether each mixture is oil or water base.

## TIPS FROM THE PROS

• Place a dot of the paint or glaze on the container lid so you can see the color of the contents easily.

It's best to store paint thinner and flammable paints (check labels) in a metal cabinet.

## LEFTOVER THINNER

Paint thinner can be stored in a sealed jar or plastic jug and reused. At the end of each work session, pour used thinner into the storage container, using a funnel to prevent spills. (Do not pour the used thinner back into the original container if it still holds unused thinner.) Label and date the container. The paint will settle overnight, and you can pour the clear thinner into a clean working container the next day. After using the same thinner for several days, don't reuse it; just keep it in the storage container. Work with fresh thinner and store it in another container. When the second thinner has been used several times, add it to the first storage container and start with clean thinner again. Continue in this manner. When the first storage container is full, dispose of it legally.

## TIPS FROM THE PROS

• Paint thinner that has been used too many times will still look clear, but it will actually have paint particles suspended in it. It will develop an unpleasant odor—when it does, it's definitely no longer useful.

## WHICH TECHNIQUE IS BEST FOR YOUR WALLS?

If you use the right materials and tools and practice your chosen technique, there is really only one thing that might stand in the way of your ability to do wonderful decorative painting, and that is the condition of the surface you plan to paint. Ideally, walls and woodwork should be in optimum condition, but this may not always be possible. Following are some hints for choosing a decorative treatment for a less-than-perfect surface. Of course, nearly every technique will look good on a surface that is in good condition.

The following techniques camouflage imperfect surfaces.
• Colorwashing
• Fresco Colorwashing
• Rubbing
• Ragging
• Spattering
• Sponging

The following techniques highlight surface flaws. Use them only on perfectly smooth surfaces.
• Dragging
• Stippling
• Combing
• Marble

# UNDERSTANDING COLOR

As you look through the materials lists in this book, you'll see the terms *base coat* and *glaze* listed repeatedly. These refer to two or more colors, one applied on top of the other. Depending on the colors and the painting technique, when the base coat and glaze are viewed in combination, they may or may not blend to make a new color. To decide which paint colors to use, you'll have to choose a "perceived," or blended, color for your work and then figure out its component colors. Expect to do lots of experimenting to work out a combination with the desired harmony or contrast. You'll want to think not only about the paint colors but about the overall use of color in the room you're going to paint.

## COLOR VOCABULARY

All decorative painting techniques feature a combination of colors or color values. Understanding color and learning to apply color theory is not really so difficult once you understand how the color wheel works. To begin, you need to know some basic terms and concepts.

### HUE

Hue is just another word for color. Royal blue, fire engine red, and bright yellow are hues, as are such softer colors as dove gray, terra-cotta, and cream.

• Each hue has a visual "temperature." Yellow, orange, and red are warm and lively; they're often referred to as advancing colors because they seem nearer than they actually are. Blue, green, and violet are cool and tranquil; they're called receding colors because they appear farther away than they actually are.

### VALUE

Value refers to the lightness or darkness of color.

• The more white in a color, the lighter the value; these colors, called tints, lie just inside the hue ring on the color wheel (shown at right).

• The more black in a color, the darker the color's value; these colors, termed shades, appear just outside the hue ring on the color wheel.

• Color with gray added is a tone.

• Adding white, black, or gray to colors to make tints, shades, or tones is called extending colors.

### INTENSITY

The degree of purity, or saturation, of color is called intensity. Although both pale pink and bright red are technically red, they differ in their intensity, or strength of color. You increase a color's intensity by adding more of the pure color; adding white, black, or the color's complement (page 36) reduces intensity. Full-intensity colors are so strong and stimulating that they're usually used only for emphasis in decorating.

## THE COLOR WHEEL

As you look at the color wheel (below), keep in mind that its colors are almost always altered and combined in ways that soften their impact. All color combinations, from safe to audacious, come from variations and combinations on the basic color wheel. Although the color wheel can't dictate formula schemes, it can help you imagine what will happen when colors are put together. If you have a definite color in mind, the color wheel expands your choices by allowing you to work out different schemes.

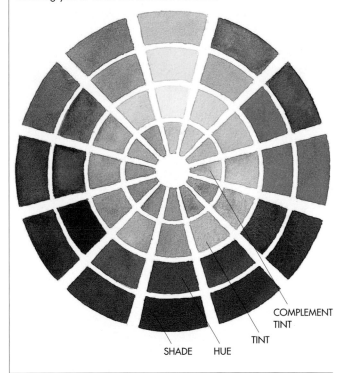

COMPLEMENT
TINT

TINT

SHADE    HUE

### PRIMARY COLORS

Red, blue, and yellow are the primary colors; they are the source of all other colors. Primaries are powerful, usually too powerful to use alone at full strength on large expanses, such as walls.

### SECONDARY COLORS

When equal parts of two primary colors are combined, secondary colors are formed: green comes from blue and yellow, orange from yellow and red, and violet from red and blue. Secondary colors lie midway between the primary colors on the color wheel; they are less strong than primaries.

## INTERMEDIATE COLORS

When a primary color is mixed with an adjacent secondary color, an intermediate color is formed: blue (a primary) and violet (a secondary) combine to make blue-violet, an intermediate.

## TERTIARY AND QUATERNARY COLORS

Subtle blends of pure color, tertiary and quaternary colors are richer hues than shades, which are made by adding black.

• Tertiary colors are formed when two secondary colors are mixed. They add depth and sophistication to a color scheme. Look at the color circle (below) and follow the arrows to make the tertiaries: green and orange make wheat; orange and violet make brick; and violet and green make slate. Note that the tertiaries shown have had varying amounts of white added to them.

• Quaternary colors are formed when two tertiary colors are mixed: wheat and brick become sandstone, brick and slate become eggplant, and slate and wheat become juniper.

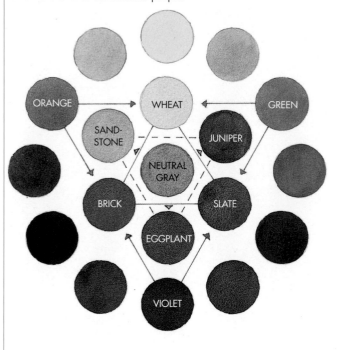

## COMPLEMENTARY COLORS

Colors that lie opposite each other on the color wheel are known as complementary colors. Red and green are complements, as are blue and orange, yellow and violet. Complementary colors are stimulating and full of surprises.

• Used in their full intensity, they seem harsh. When mixed in equal amounts, they neutralize each other, forming a flat, neutral gray.

• When a small amount of one color is added to its complement, the result is a pleasing, less intense version of the predominant color. The inner wedges on the color wheel (page 35) show tints that have a bit of complement added, forming extended and neutralized colors.

## COLOR COMBINATIONS

Once you see how the different color combinations are formed, you can build your own combinations from a favorite color or colors. You don't have to think of colors in their full intensities. By neutralizing them (adding a bit of a color's complement) and extending them (adding white, black, or gray), you'll change the character of colors and form more sophisticated combinations.

## MONOCHROMATIC

Monochromatic schemes—combinations that employ one color in a variety of intensities and values—are simple to put together and easy to live with because they're so restful. Since colors have so much in common in monochromatic schemes, rooms appear unified and harmonious. Contrasting values will create interest, but too much variation may look uneven.

## COMPLEMENTARY

Based on any two colors opposite each other on the color wheel, complementary schemes are richer than monochromatic ones because they balance warm and cool colors. Depending upon the hues, these combinations can be startling or subdued. Look beyond such obviously jarring complements as intense yellow and violet to see the possibilities of quiet combinations such as cream and amethyst (tints of yellow and violet, each slightly neutralized).

• A triad combination consists of any three colors equidistant from each other on the color wheel.

• A split complement also contains three colors—one primary or intermediate color plus the color on each side of its opposite. Yellow plus red-violet and blue-violet is one example of a split complement.

• A double split complement comes from splitting both sides of the color wheel, resulting in a four-color scheme.

## ANALOGOUS

Varied yet harmonious, analogous, or related, color combinations are composed of two or more colors that lie next to each other on the color wheel. The most agreeable analogous combinations are limited to colors falling between two primaries and including one of those primaries—yellow-green, green, blue-green, and blue, for example. Note that every hue contains at least a touch of the primary color.

*Intense colors add drama to a decor. In this sitting room the bold choice of deep red walls sets off richly textured furnishings. The walls were first rubbed with a red glaze and then randomly stenciled all over with a leaf pattern. The slightly lighter red of the leaves tones down the potentially overwhelming color. The sponged chair rail, dado, and mantel, along with the fanciful trompe l'oeil crown molding, add opulence and contrast.*

*A blue and white color scheme is cool, crisp, and restful. Colorwashing over plaster walls lends an informal touch to the grand proportions of this room. The white trim has been hand-painted to resemble a weathered crackle finish, bringing the lovely architectural details into prominence. Red pillows tossed on the sofa break up the blue and add some warmth to the room.*

Colors have qualities that can work magic on walls. Understanding the characteristics of color will open up a world of design ideas and make it easier for you to choose the right paint colors for your room.

### HOW LIGHT AFFECTS COLOR

The quality of light, whether natural or artificial, can greatly affect colors. That is why it's so important to examine a large sample of the decorative technique you've selected in the colors you think you want under different light conditions.

• Cool fluorescent light amplifies cool colors and weakens warm ones: under cool light, blue seems more blue, but yellow appears duller. Warm incandescent light enhances warm colors while weakening cool ones.

• Reflected light behaves in much the same way. Light bouncing off a cool green lawn into a room, for example, will have a different effect than light reflecting off a warm brick wall. Light tinted with a certain color will raise the intensity of similar colors and neutralize complementary colors.

• Light also alters a color's value. Low light darkens value and reduces intensity; a higher light level lightens value and increases intensity. Too much light can make colors look washed out.

### ALTERING SPACE WITH COLOR

A color's visual temperature can alter the sense of space in a room.

• Warm colors, such as apricot, yellow, and terra-cotta, appear to advance. Walls finished in these colors seem closer, making the room appear smaller. You can easily take advantage of this to make a large room feel more intimate.

• Blue, green, and violet, on the other hand, are cool, serene hues that seem to recede. Walls painted these colors tend to make a room appear more spacious than it really is.

• Intensity and value also play a role in altering the perception of room size. More intense colors make a room seem smaller, while low-intensity colors visually increase the sense of space. Darker values (shades) diminish room size because they absorb light. Unbroken expanses of very light values reflect the light and open up space.

• Whatever the colors, intensities, or values, a great deal of contrast has the same impact as a dark color—it reduces the perceived space. Conversely, monochromatic and analogous schemes have the tendency to enlarge space. Neutrals of similar value also seem to make walls retreat, allowing the emphasis to fall on furnishings.

The photographs on these pages show how different hues of the same color can have entirely different effects.

Above: Exotic objets d'art are enhanced by a dramatic backdrop. The use of only two colors—brilliant peacock and marigold— helps to unify the disparate objects and furniture styles. The walls and mantel have been ragged with cheesecloth, which adds texture and interest to the colors.

Opposite, top: Walls ragged and then softened in a seafoamy blue-green seem to recede, making this narrow hallway feel more spacious. The hand-painted faux tile border complements the strong designs of the furnishings and artwork.

Opposite, bottom: This unusual paint treatment is lively and contemporary, but several values of aqua make the overall effect quite restful. Torn scraps of gold leaf were scattered over the walls, which were then sponged. The mustard woodwork was dragged with aqua and white, then decorated with gold leaf and stenciled blue triangles.

FACE

The effects that can be created with decorative painting are virtually infinite. You can add a translucent wash of color to a wall, applying it in a uniform haze or with clouds and swirls of varying intensity. You can paint stripes, create a pattern of fine or coarse lines with a comb or brush, make an allover imprint with a crushed rag or a sponge, or spatter flecks of paint. You can use these techniques alone or together, applying light colors over dark, or dark over light, working with a subtle palette or one with great contrast. And you can transform plain walls or woodwork with a faux finish such as Marble, Malachite, or Mahogany, adding luxury or character where none exists.

Each technique in this chapter is introduced with inspirational photos of painted interiors. The directions begin with a list of materials and tools and continue with step-by-step instructions and photos. Some techniques can be worked in more than one way, each producing a different effect; where this is so, you'll find complete directions for each method. And where a slight change of color or an additional layer of glaze can alter an effect, you'll find a Variation subhead with a photo and caption explaining different approaches to try. Helpful Tips from the Pros are included throughout.

Some of the techniques are subtle and produce similar results that are difficult to distinguish in photographs. If you are unsure which will be best for you, test several to see which you prefer. Don't hesitate to combine them: the more layers of glaze you use and the more discreetly you manipulate them, the more interesting the results will be. So choose a technique, read Basics, and start painting.

**TECHNIQUES**

One of the simplest decorative painting techniques, Colorwashing is informal and airy; depending on the colors used, it can create a lively, rustic, or pastoral atmosphere. It's done with a transparent glaze and, because it has a textured appearance that hides flaws, is ideal for walls that are not in good condition. You can use one or more glaze colors for Colorwashing, brushing them loosely over a contrasting background. For a more rustic look, first add a plaster skim coat to the walls and then colorwash (see Fresco Colorwashing, page 46).

## TOOLS
Paint bucket, rack, brushes, and roller for base coat
3" brown paper painter's tape
Latex gloves
Mixing bucket
Stir sticks
Paint tray with tray liner
3" house painter's brush
Paper towels or rags for cleanup

## BASE COAT
Latex satin paint

## GLAZE
1 part alkyd paint
1 part alkyd glazing liquid
1 part paint thinner
Small amount of linseed oil

*Or commercially prepared glaze or Latex or Acrylic Glaze (page 16), thinned*

*We used light grass green for the base; deep grass green for the glaze.*

*Before you begin, read Basics, pages 7–39.*

*Immediately submerge oil- or solvent-soiled rags in water. Discard according to local ordinances.*

*Right: Colorwashing is perhaps an unexpected choice for formal architecture, but it can be an effective and dramatic background for ornate moldings and opulent accessories. Below: Gold-hued walls colorwashed with burnt orange have a rich and antique look. Bottom: Softened peach-on-peach Colorwashing appears pretty and restful. Note also the stenciled chair rail.*

# COLORWASHING

**1** Apply the base coat and let it dry for 2 days.

**2** Mask the ceiling, baseboard, and walls adjacent to where you'll be working. Mix the glaze; it should have the consistency of buttermilk. Pour some of the glaze into the paint tray.

**3** Beginning near the top corner, loosely brush the glaze onto the wall in random, crisscross strokes, leaving some of the base coat exposed. Stop the brush strokes several inches from the top or side corners and, using the same brush, work the glaze into and away from the corner. Cover an area about

3' in diameter. Blend in the strokes by lightly and repeatedly going over the area with the brush. Also see Handling Corners, page 26.

### TIPS FROM THE PROS

• Your brush strokes can be crude as you apply the glaze, but keep an eye out for drips and immediately brush them out.

**4** Repeat, starting below the area you just covered. Be sure to blend your strokes into the previously covered area.

**5** Repeat, working alternately next to and below the area just completed, until the wall is done.

### TIPS FROM THE PROS

• To minimize demarcation lines between the areas of application, work with a partner, each of you working along different edges.

**6** The completed Colorwashing is light and airy, with evident brush strokes that make the effect informal, even rustic.

## VARIATIONS

• To create a cloudlike effect with extra depth, intersperse white or off-white and colored glazes. In order to blend the colors together, you have to apply both at the same time, so work with a brush in each hand or have a second person apply one color (also read steps 7 and 8 on page 48). Here the base coat and green glaze are the same as in the previous sample, but blended with off-white.

• Here an antique effect simulating fresco without the plaster has been created by washing two ochre tones over a cream base coat. The effect is further aged with interspersed soft blue accents. The painting is full of cloudlike swirls. On a large wall, consider concentrating more of one tone in some areas, another tone in other areas. Experiment to find a pleasing accent color.

• You can also wash a light color over a dark background. Here pale blue has been brushed loosely over a deep sapphire base coat to create a wonderful evening sky. Not all color combinations work this way—we tried to reverse our green pair and the results were not at all appealing—so experiment before committing to a particular palette.

*Green trim frames yellow Colorwashing in this country dining room. The deep hue of the moldings balances the dark furnishings and makes the setting harmonious and quiet. Yellow ochre tones are perennially popular for Colorwashing. Compare their effect here with the photo on page 43—different, but equally appealing.*

Give your decor a head start on an Old World look by applying a skim coat of joint compound to your walls before you colorwash them. An uneven surface is the goal, so this technique is not as tricky as you might think—though you may find it tedious if you are covering a large area. The compound need not be applied all at once; you can add on next to a dry section. Once the skim coat is in place, apply a water-base primer, then use a latex base coat to set up a surface that is slightly absorbent. This will give the final effect a chalkier look. Here we colorwashed with two colors, but you can use as many as you like.

*Right: Buff tones colorwashed over rough plaster are the perfect complement to these rustic beams.*
*Below: After this wall was colorwashed, the crevices between sections of the plaster skim coat were accented with a dark glaze.*
*Bottom: A plaster skim coat, applied in large, rough arcs and then colorwashed, pairs charmingly with distressed cabinets to provide a country farmhouse ambience.*

## TOOLS

Wide spackling knife
Joint compound
Plasterer's trough or other small container
Paint bucket, rack, brushes, and high-nap paint rollers for primer and base coat
Curved painter's tool
3" brown paper painter's tape
Latex gloves
Mixing buckets
Stir sticks
Paint trays with tray liners
2" foam brush(es)
3" house painter's brush(es)
Paper towels or rags for cleanup

## PRIMER

Water-base primer

## BASE COAT

Latex eggshell paint

## GLAZE

1 part alkyd paint
1 part alkyd glazing liquid
1–2 parts paint thinner
Small amount of linseed oil

*Or commercially prepared glaze or Latex or Acrylic Glaze (page 16), thinned*

*We used very pale aqua for the base; medium aqua and peacock for the glazes.*

*Before you begin, read Basics, pages 7–39. Also read Colorwashing, pages 42–45.*

*Immediately submerge oil- or solvent-soiled rags in water. Discard according to local ordinances.*

# FRESCO COLORWASHING

**1** If your walls have never been painted, prime them and allow the primer to dry as recommended by the manufacturer.

**2** Using the spackling knife, transfer some of the joint compound to the plasterer's trough. Dip the spackling knife into the compound and scoop up about ⅔ cup. Starting at an upper corner, hold the knife with the compound-filled side flat against the wall and drag it lightly either downward or sideways, off-loading the compound. Spread the compound about ⅜" thick and leave the surface rough.

**3** Reload the spackling knife and repeat, starting adjacent to the section you just completed, laying on the compound in a random, sweeping motion to create crevices.

**TIPS FROM THE PROS**

• Keep the compound surface fairly thin. A large buildup of compound could result in later cracking.

• The compound begins to harden quite quickly, so immediately manipulate each knifeful to the desired texture.

• Clean tools immediately with water and dry them with a rag.

**4** Let the compound dry. (You'll know it's dry when it's no longer cool to the touch.) Sand any harsh peaks. Vacuum gently to remove plaster dust. Apply one coat of primer using the high-nap roller. Let it dry for 1–2 days, depending on the weather.

**5** Apply the base coat using a clean high-nap roller. Let it dry for 2 days.

**6** Mask the ceiling, baseboard, and walls adjacent to where you'll begin. Mix one or more colors of glaze. The glazes should have the consistency of buttermilk. Pour some of each glaze into a paint tray.

**7** Beginning near one top corner and using a paintbrush, brush some of one color glaze onto the wall in random, crisscross strokes. Using a second paintbrush, loosely brush some of the second color glaze onto a nearby area. Leave some of the base coat exposed and cover an area 2'–3' in diameter.

Spread the glazes by lightly going over the area with the brushes. Also see Handling Corners, page 26.

**TIPS FROM THE PROS**

• Your brush strokes can be crude as you apply the glaze, but keep an eye out for drips and immediately brush them out.

**8** To blend the glazes, stroke repeatedly with the brush or rotate the brush against the wall to rub the glaze in. Add more of each color to the wall below the area you just covered. Be sure to blend your strokes into the previously covered area.

## TIPS FROM THE PROS

• Some of the glaze will soak into the latex base coat, so start by applying less rather than more glaze and experiment to see how long it stays workable enough for you to spread and blend it to achieve the effect you want.

• If you like, you can rub portions of the glaze with a jersey or cheesecloth rag. You can also add more glaze to some areas to emphasize the texture.

**9** Repeat, working alternately next to and below the area just completed, until the wall is done.

## TIPS FROM THE PROS

• To minimize demarcation lines between the areas of application, work with a partner, each of you working along different edges.

**10** The pale colors impart a light and airy look even to rustic plaster; another palette might evoke an era of antiquity. Note how some of the glaze has been caught in the plaster crevices.

Add more interest to Fresco Colorwashing by applying a pattern. You can use a stencil or, as we did, dot the surface with rubber stamp motifs. Whichever you choose, the image will be soft because of the irregular surface. Acrylic paints work fine. Here we used a medium blue, the deep peacock used for the Colorwashing, and a metallic silver. Read Stamping, pages 92–95, for more information.

**R**ubbed glazes are ideal for less-than-perfect walls. The imperfections may even enhance the charm of this technique. There are two methods by which you can rub glaze over a surface—on or off. For Rubbing On, you dip a rag into glaze and simply rub it on top of the base coat, creating a light, translucent effect quite similar to Colorwashing but without the brush strokes. For Rubbing Off, you brush the glaze onto the painted surface and then remove it with a rag. The glaze is thicker than that used in Rubbing On, so the color is more intense and more opaque. Both techniques create swirled clouds of color.

*Right: This eclectic contemporary decor is subtle and elegant, with ecru rubbed-off walls that echo the colors in the sponged sideboard.*
*Below: A moss-colored glaze rubbed onto the walls enhances the comfortable ambience of this room; the effect is interesting but not at all fussy.*
*Left: A close-up view of Rubbing Off in tones of peach on peach.*

### TOOLS

Paint bucket, rack, brushes, and roller for base coat
3" brown paper painter's tape
Box of jersey knit rags
Latex gloves
Mixing bucket
Stir sticks
Paint tray with tray liner
2" foam paintbrush (for Rubbing On only)
3" house painter's brush
Paper towels or rags for cleanup

### For Rubbing On
**BASE COAT**

Latex or alkyd satin paint

### GLAZE

1 part alkyd paint
1 part alkyd glazing liquid
2 parts paint thinner
Small amount of linseed oil

*Or commercially prepared glaze or Latex or Acrylic Glaze (page 16)*

*We used light blue for the base; medium blue for the glaze.*

*Before you begin either method, read Basics, pages 7–39.*

*Immediately submerge oil- or solvent-soiled rags in water. Discard according to local ordinances.*

### For Rubbing Off
**BASE COAT**

Latex satin paint

### GLAZE

1 part alkyd paint
1 part glazing liquid
1 part paint thinner
Small amount of linseed oil

*Or commercially prepared glaze or Latex or Acrylic Glaze (page 16)*

*We used pale peach for the base; medium peach for the glaze.*

### TIPS FOR RUBBING

• You don't have to worry about maintaining a wet edge with either rubbing method, and you don't have to mask adjacent walls.
• For Rubbing Off, you'll have better results with two people working side by side: one to brush on the glaze and one to rub it off. This will ensure that the applied glaze is as wet as possible while you're rubbing.

# RUBBING ON

**1** Apply the base coat and let it dry, 2 days for latex, 2–3 days for alkyd.

**2** Using the jersey rags, prepare several bolster rags (see Basics, page 12).

**3** Mask the ceilings and baseboards. Mix the glaze; it should have the consistency of heavy cream. Pour some of the glaze into the paint tray.

**4** Starting from the ceiling and working down to the baseboard, apply glaze with the foam paintbrush to both walls in one corner; reload the brush as needed. Using the bolster rag, rub the glaze so that it fades out from the corner toward the center of each wall. Pull out any remaining glaze in the corner by pouncing with the house painter's brush. Also see Handling Corners, page 27.

**5** Dip the bolster rag into the glaze and dab off the excess on the track of the paint tray.

**6** Place the bolster rag on the wall about 1' away from the rubbed corner. Using small circular movements, rub the glaze toward the corner, fading the new glaze into the edges of the previously rubbed section. Continue spreading the glaze out in all directions until all the glaze on your rag is faded 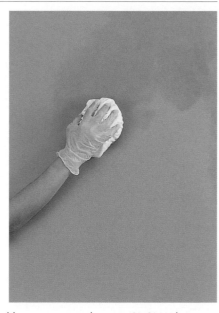 into the wall; you should cover an irregular area 2'–3' in diameter. Note that the edges will be lighter than the center where you first placed the bolster.

**7** Repeat, working beneath the previous section and fading the glaze into it.

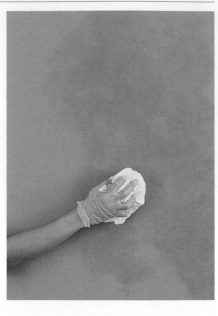

**8** Continue to repeat, alternating between working next to and beneath each previously rubbed section.

**TIPS FROM THE PROS**
• When you're blending into more than one adjacent area, don't try to refine one edge at a time. Instead, develop a rhythm for lifting the bolster and working back and forth between the previously worked edges.

**9** Notice how the areas of deeper color gradually blend into areas of faded-out color.

If you rub a light glaze over a deeper base color, you'll have a surface with a chalky look. Here pale blue glaze was rubbed over the same medium blue base used in the previous sample.

*A medium blue glaze rubbed onto pale blue walls leaves subtle swirls of color as fresh as a summer sky—a wonderful choice to pair with white furnishings.*

# RUBBING OFF

**1** Apply the base coat and let it dry, 2 days for latex, 2–3 days for alkyd.

**2** Using the jersey rags, prepare several bolster rags (see Basics, page 12).

**3** Mask the ceiling and baseboard. Mix the glaze; it should have the consistency of pancake batter. Pour some of the glaze into the paint tray.

**4** Starting at the ceiling, cut in the glaze in one corner with the house painter's brush (see Basics, page 23); extend the glaze slightly onto the adjacent wall. Using the bolster rag, rub the glaze off both walls using small circular movements to fade out the edges. Use the brush to pounce out any glaze that has accumulated in the corner. Also see Handling Corners, page 26.

**5** Starting near the top corner on one wall, brush on some glaze using crisscross strokes. Cover an irregular area about 2' in diameter, and leave a gap of 6"–12" between the rubbed corner and new section.

**6** Rub off the glaze, fading out into the adjacent areas.

**7** Repeat, alternating between working next to and beneath each previously rubbed section.

### TIPS FROM THE PROS

• When you're blending into more than one adjacent area, don't try to refine one edge at a time. Instead, develop a rhythm for lifting the bolster and working in and out of the painted glaze, back and forth between the previously worked edges.

**8** Notice that Rubbing Off gives you a more blended look than Rubbing On. Also, because you start off with more paint on the wall, less of the base coat shows through.

# S T I P P L I N G

**S**tippling is a subtle painting technique that leaves a nearly imperceptible texture in an allover glaze. The effect is suedelike, with a haze of color gracing the base coat. Three stippling methods are explained here. The first is done with a stippling brush (this looks like a small push broom without the handle), which is tapped repeatedly onto a wet glaze to remove some of the color. A softer, subtler, easier version of Stippling can be done with cheesecloth. A third, extremely subtle Stippling effect can be created by rolling off the glaze with a special foam roller.

*Below: The effect of Stippling is so subtle that even when the glaze is very different from the base color, you must be quite close before you see the contrasting colors. Here bright peacock was stippled with a brush over pale green. Bottom: The soft, cheesecloth-stippled walls form a graceful backdrop to this magnificent fireplace. Background: A close-up view of medium mauve stippled with a brush over pale mauve.*

## TOOLS

Paint bucket, rack, brushes, and roller for base coat

3" brown paper painter's tape

Latex gloves

Mixing bucket

Stir sticks

Paint tray with tray liner

9" low-nap roller with handle

Curved painter's tool

2" foam brush

3" house painter's brush

Paper towels or rags for cleanup

## ADDITIONAL TOOLS (DEPENDING ON THE TECHNIQUE):

Stippling brush

Cheesecloth

2 or more foam hot-dog rollers with handles

## BASE COAT

Latex or alkyd satin paint

## GLAZE

1 part alkyd paint

1 part alkyd glazing liquid

1–2 parts paint thinner or mineral spirits

Small amount of linseed oil

*Or commercially prepared glaze or Latex or Acrylic Glaze (page 16), thinned*

*We used* very pale mauve for the base; medium mauve for the glaze.

## TIPS FOR STIPPLING

• Stippling highlights every flaw, so make sure your walls are in good condition.

• Water-base glazes are likely to dry before you can successfully stipple a large area with a brush.

• You'll have better results with two people working together: one to roll on the glaze and one to stipple it. Set aside the time to do an entire wall in one session so that the leading edge will be wet when you paint each adjacent section.

*Before you begin, read Basics, pages 7–39.*

*Immediately submerge oil- or solvent-soiled rags in water. Discard according to local ordinances.*

# STIPPLING WITH A BRUSH

**1** Apply the base coat and let it dry, 2 days for latex, 2–3 days for alkyd.

**2** Mask the ceiling, baseboard, and walls adjacent to where you'll be working. Mix the glaze; it should have the consistency of milk. Pour some of the glaze into the paint tray.

**3** Using the foam brush, cut the glaze into the corner where you'll begin; also cut in 18" along the ceiling. Load the roller with glaze; remove the excess with the curved painter's tool. Roll two roller widths of glaze from top to bottom; reload as needed. Stop rolling 1"–2" above the baseboard; you'll move the glaze onto that area when you stipple. Also see Handling Corners, page 27.

**4** Starting in the top corner and working your way out and down, use the stippling brush to pounce off the glaze. Hold the brush so that the bristle tips tap straight onto the wall, and quickly move the brush on and off. Pounce over the stippled section repeatedly to create a suedelike surface. Do not stipple the leading edge.

**5** As your brush becomes loaded with glaze, wipe it with a clean rag.

## TIPS FROM THE PROS

- To make the stippling go faster, first remove some of the glaze by brushing over it with a paintbrush; brush over only the portion of the glaze you are about to stipple.
- If the glaze drips, don't worry. You'll pounce it off.
- Keep the stippling brush moving in the same direction with each pass over the stippled section—either side to side or up and down—then rotate the brush to a different angle for the next pass.
- The more you pounce over the area, the more transparent the top color will become.

**6** Cut in another 18" section along the ceiling adjacent to the first section. Roll two roller widths of glaze from top to bottom, reloading as needed. Working from the top to the bottom in one pass, pounce off the glaze along the edge of the previously stippled section; this will prevent a demarcation line

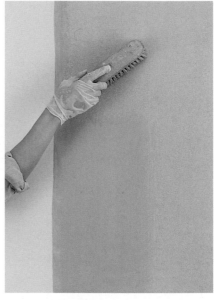

from forming. When you reach the baseboard, move to the top of the fresh glaze and continue as before.

**7** The completed effect has a finely dappled surface with an allover translucent haze of color.

## STIPPLING WITH CHEESECLOTH

**1** If your cheesecloth is one length, cut it into pieces about 2' square. Make several bolster rags (see Basics, page 12).

**2** Read the complete directions for Stippling with a Brush, opposite. Complete steps 1–3.

**3** Starting in the top corner and working your way out and down, pounce off the glaze by moving the bolster rag straight on and off the wall. Periodically blot the bolster on a rag. Do not stipple the leading edge.

**4** Change the outer layer of the bolster rag as it becomes saturated with paint. Continue, following steps 6 and 7 of Stippling with a Brush, opposite, but using the cheesecloth.

**5** The cheesecloth produces a finer haze of color than the stippling brush.

*Here a vibrant flame glaze was stippled with cheesecloth over a pale orange wall and then given a high-gloss varnish to make a rich background for formal furnishings. Note the fantasy marble baseboard and stylized faux marquetry floor.*

# STIPPLING WITH A FOAM ROLLER

**1** Read the complete directions for Stippling with a Brush, page 56. Complete steps 1 and 2.

**2** Using the house painter's brush lightly loaded with glaze, cut in the glaze for about 18" along the ceiling and baseboard. Load a hot-dog roller with glaze. Do not scrape off any of the glaze. Roll the glaze from ceiling to baseboard along the corner, rerolling the area until you fill it in completely. Repeat to fill the rest of the cut-in area.

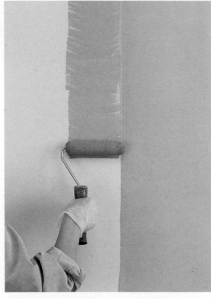

**3** Using a clean hot-dog roller, lightly roll over the glaze. Keep rolling over the same area until you remove enough glaze to produce the desired effect. When the roller becomes loaded with glaze, blot it by rolling it over a paper towel.

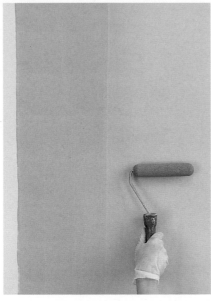

### TIPS FROM THE PROS

• To avoid a demarcation line, don't lift your roller partway down the wall; always roll continuously from ceiling to baseboard.

• As you work, blot the rollers frequently so that you'll always have a clean one available to remove the glaze.

**4** Starting adjacent to the area you just rolled, cut in and roll glaze onto another section. Blend the glaze into the previously rolled section. Reload the roller as needed. Roll off the glaze with a clean roller. Repeat until the wall is completed.

**5** The hot-dog roller produces a finer haze of color than the cheesecloth. Used alone, this technique produces walls that are just one step removed from solid color. Used over another, more active paint finish, it can subdue and even rescue an effect that is too busy or too bright.

**T**raditional ragged walls have the look of crushed velvet or soft suede. To rag, you repeatedly pounce a wadded paper towel or cloth onto a wet allover glaze, removing some of the color and leaving many impressions of the rag. The effect varies with the colors used and the amount of glaze removed. A bolder effect can be achieved by pressing a sheet of plastic onto the wet glaze, while a controlled crosshatch pattern can be created if you remove the glaze with a scrunched pleated piece of plastic.

*Below: Eccentric painting sets the stage in this contemporary bedroom. A brick-colored glaze was brushed horizontally across the walls, then removed with vertically held scrunched plastic.*
*Bottom: Classic ragging in tomato red is rich and lively.*
*Background: A close-up view of Classic Ragging in celadon over seafoam.*

## TOOLS

Paint bucket, rack, brushes, and roller for base coat
3" brown paper painter's tape
Latex gloves
Mixing bucket
Stir sticks
Paint tray with tray liner
2" foam brush
9" low-nap roller and handle
Curved painter's tool
3" house painter's brush
Paper towel roll(s)
Paper towels or rags for cleanup

### For Plastic or Crosshatch Ragging
ADDITIONAL TOOLS

Roll of professional painter's plastic (1.5 mil) or a lightweight plastic drop cloth

## BASE COAT

Latex or alkyd satin paint

## GLAZE

1 part alkyd paint
1 part alkyd glazing liquid
1 part paint thinner or mineral spirits
Small amount of linseed oil

*Or* commercially prepared glaze or Latex or Acrylic Glaze (see page 16)

*We used* very pale seafoam for the base; soft celadon for the glaze.

## TIPS FOR RAGGING

• You'll get better results with two people working side by side: one to brush on the glaze and one to rag it off. Set aside the time to do an entire wall in one session so that the leading edge will be wet when you paint the adjacent section.

• You don't need fine finger control for ragging, so wear heavy-duty work gloves. These gloves slide on and off easily, allowing you to tear off and wad paper towel rags as needed.

*Before you begin, read Basics, pages 7–39.*

*Immediately submerge oil- or solvent-soiled rags in water. Discard according to local ordinances.*

# CLASSIC RAGGING

**1** Apply the base coat and let it dry, 2 days for latex, 2–3 days for alkyd.

**2** Mask the ceiling, baseboard, and walls adjacent to where you'll be working. Mix the glaze; it should have the consistency of heavy cream. Pour some of the glaze into the paint tray.

**3** Tear off about 10 five-towel lengths of paper towels. Wad up one length of paper towel to be your first "rag" and keep the others nearby.

**4** Using the foam brush, cut the glaze into the corner where you'll begin; also cut in for 18" along the ceiling and baseboard. Load the roller with glaze; remove the excess with the curved painter's tool. Roll two roller widths of glaze from top to bottom; reload as needed.

**5** Beginning in the corner and working from top to bottom, pounce the rag on the wet glaze, using quick movements of your wrist. Working in an area approximately 2' deep, space the dabs 3"–6" apart; don't work onto the leading edge. Continue to dab in between the first set of dabs until you've filled all the spaces. Vary the painted print by alternately rotating and rearranging the rag after lifting it. When the rag becomes saturated with glaze, change to a fresh one. Do not rag the leading edge.

**TIPS FROM THE PROS**
• Bunch the rag as necessary so that it fits into the ceiling and vertical corners. Also see Handling Corners, page 26.

**6** Repeat, ragging beneath the previously worked area, until you reach the baseboard.

**TIPS FROM THE PROS**
• Be careful not to rotate the rag on the surface, or the glaze will smear.
• Rework the same area as much as you need to make the ragged pattern even; the color should be uniform, not variously light or dark.
• Ragged patterns have more definition when dry than while wet.

**7** Cut in another 18" section along the ceiling and baseboard adjacent to the first section. Roll two roller widths of glaze from top to bottom, reloading as needed.

**8** Continue ragging, pouncing from ceiling to floor along the edge of the previous section to blend it with the fresh glaze; then rag the width of glaze from ceiling to floor, working in 2'-deep sections as before.

**TIPS FROM THE PROS**
• Change your rag when it becomes saturated with paint. Be sure to start with a fresh rag at the ceiling to make a smooth transition.

**9** When completed, Classic Ragging has an even texture. It can provide a good background for stronger patterns, which you can see in the Damask Stencil Variation on page 101.

see in the Damask Stencil Variation on page 101.

## VARIATION

• For a softer look, gently stroke the tip of a 3" paintbrush over the ragged-off area in a haphazard fashion. Do this immediately after ragging each section.

# PLASTIC RAGGING

**1** Cut several pieces of painter's plastic 18"–24" square. Complete steps 1, 2, and 4 of Classic Ragging, opposite.

**2** Beginning at the ceiling, place a piece of plastic over the glaze. Press down lightly in random areas and peel off. Reposition the plastic below the area just pressed and repeat.

**3** When the plastic becomes saturated, discard and replace it. You can reposition the plastic over the same area and press again to even out the effect. Continue to rag the applied glaze.

**4** Cut in another 18" section along the ceiling and baseboard adjacent to the first section. Roll two roller widths of glaze from top to bottom, reloading as needed. Rag with plastic as before. Continue in this manner until the wall is complete.

**5** The completed Plastic Ragging is bolder than Classic Ragging. By the way, it looks much messier to do than it really is.

# CROSSHATCH RAGGING

**1** Cut several pieces of painter's plastic about 18" square. Complete steps 1, 2, and 4 of Classic Ragging, page 60.

**TIPS FROM THE PROS**

• Practice this technique to see how large a piece of plastic you feel comfortable working with, then cut several pieces in that size.

**2** Hold one piece of plastic taut in both hands and scrunch it up from top to bottom. Adjust your grip so that you can keep the plastic taut and scrunched while working with it.

**3** Hold the scrunched plastic parallel to the ceiling and pounce it down the wet glaze from ceiling to baseboard. When the plastic becomes saturated, rotate it or change to a new piece. Return to the ceiling and pounce the next area in the same manner, but don't pounce into the leading edge.

**4** Hold the scrunched plastic perpendicular to the ceiling and, beginning at the ceiling in the corner, pounce it horizontally across the previously pounced glaze to create a crosshatch pattern. Then reposition the plastic beneath this section and repeat.

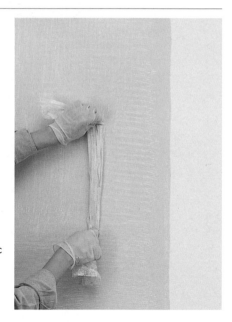

**5** Repeat until you reach the baseboard. Then cut in another 18" section along the ceiling and baseboard adjacent to the first section. Roll two roller widths of glaze from top to bottom, reloading as needed. Rag with scrunched plastic as before. Continue in this manner until the wall is complete.

**6** When completed, Crosshatch Ragging resembles grass cloth. It's a good choice for a decor with a retro or island theme.

*This bathroom features walls with a burnt gold glaze ragged over a pale yellow base. Because the ragging was softened with a dry brush, it doesn't compete with the stained glass window; see the Variation on page 61 for softening directions.*

**R**ag Rolling is a more challenging and time-consuming technique than Ragging, and the pattern created is more controlled and linear. For Rag Rolling, you first apply glaze to a painted surface, then remove part of it by rolling a twisted rag from ceiling to baseboard. This technique is most often done with a light base and deeper glaze, but some colors work well layered light over dark.

*Below: Rolling a short rag in random directions breaks up the linear pattern of traditional Rag Rolling.*
*Bottom: Light and dark rag-rolled lavender stripes emphasize the tall windows and high ceilings of this bedroom.*

### TOOLS

Paint bucket, rack, brushes, and roller for base coat
3" brown paper painter's tape
Latex gloves
Mixing bucket
Stir sticks
Paint tray with tray liner
9" low-nap roller with handle
Curved painter's tool
2" foam brush
3" house painter's brush
Jersey knit rags
Paper towels or rags for cleanup

### BASE COAT

Latex or alkyd satin paint

### GLAZE

1 part alkyd paint
1 part alkyd glazing liquid
2 parts paint thinner or mineral spirits
Small amount of linseed oil

*Or* commercially prepared glaze or Latex or Acrylic Glaze (page 16)

*We used* pale coral for the base; deeper coral for the glaze.

### TIPS FOR RAG ROLLING

• You'll get better results with two people working side by side: one to roll on the glaze with a roller and one to roll it off with a rag. Set aside the time to do an entire wall in one session so that the leading edge will be wet when you paint each adjacent section.

*Before you begin, read Basics, pages 7–39.*

*Immediately submerge oil- or solvent-soiled rags in water. Discard according to local ordinances.*

# RAG ROLLING

**1** Apply the base coat and let it dry, 2 days for latex, 2–3 days for alkyd.

**2** Mask the walls, ceilings, and baseboards adjacent to where you'll be working. Mix the glaze; it should have the consistency of heavy cream. Pour some of the glaze into the paint tray.

**3** Cut in the first corner (refer to Basics, page 22); start at the ceiling and use the foam brush to apply the glaze. Also cut in for 18" along the ceiling and baseboard. Load the roller with glaze; remove the excess with the curved painter's tool. Roll two roller widths of glaze from top to bottom; reload as needed.

**4** Fold a rag in half and twist lengthwise, forming a long loose cylinder.

**TIPS FROM THE PROS**
• Most packaged rags are about 2' square. If this size makes a roll that is too long for you to handle comfortably, cut them down.

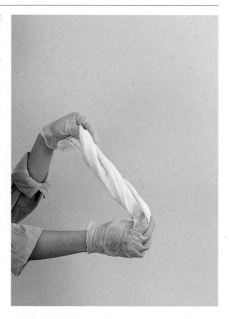

**5** Place the rag at the top of the wall, aligning one end with the corner. Using your fingertips, roll the rag down the wall, working your way to the baseboard; be sure the roll does not extend all the way to the leading edge. When the rag stops removing glaze, retwist it to reveal a clean area. When it becomes saturated, switch to a clean rag. Also see Handling Corners, page 26.

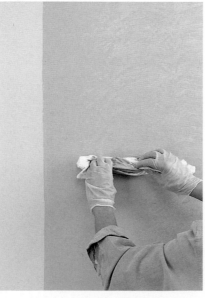

**TIPS FROM THE PROS**
• You don't have to roll the rag in one continuous motion from top to bottom. You can lift it, rearrange the roll, and reposition it whenever you like.
• If the pattern appears uneven, retouch it by pouncing small areas lightly with the rolled rag.

**6** Cut in another 18" section along the ceiling and baseboard adjacent to the first section. Roll two roller widths of glaze from top to bottom, reloading as needed.

**7** Roll your rag from ceiling to floor through the glaze, overlapping the previously rolled section.

**8** The finished surface has a linear pattern, almost like an informal watermark. Notice that you can see where one roll ends and the next begins.

• For a looser, more open pattern, roll off the glaze with a chamois cloth. (Chamois cloth is thick double-napped flannel; you can buy it from a tailor's supplier or use rags from heavy flannel shirts.) Cut the cloth on the bias and dampen it before rolling into a cylinder.

• The surface appears airier and more open when the values of the corals are reversed—shown here rolled with jersey, not chamois.

### TIPS FROM THE PROS

• Another thing you might try is rolling diagonally instead of vertically. This will create a fantasy marble effect.

*Walls rag rolled in ice cream parlor pink are lively and cheerful. Don't discount this technique for intimate spaces such as bath and dressing rooms. Even though it's busy, it won't necessarily overwhelm, especially if the colors are light or close in value.*

**S**ponging is one of the easiest and quickest methods of decorative painting. For the most common sponging process, Sponging On, you use a large sea sponge to dab a glaze onto a painted surface, creating a lively flecked effect. The result can be either subtle or dramatic, depending on the hue and number of colors you apply. For Sponging Off, a related but quieter technique, you first roll the glaze over a painted surface and then lift off some of the wet glaze with the sponge. Sponging Off creates a subtle and softly dappled surface—a little stronger than Stippling.

*Right: Walls with two values of rose sponged on over a creamy base perfectly complement this traditional decor. Center: A top layer of softened Colorwashing adds sophistication to walls sponged with uneven layers of warm sandy hues. Bottom: At first glance these walls appear antique, but they're just lightly sponged with a terra-cotta glaze over a yellow base. Left: A close-up view of medium gold sponged on over pale gold.*

### TOOLS

Paint bucket, rack, brushes, and roller for base coat

3" brown paper painter's tape

Latex gloves

Mixing bucket

Stir sticks

Paint tray with tray liner

Large sea sponge with medium pores

Paper towels or rags for cleanup

### For Sponging On
### ADDITIONAL TOOLS

Bucket of water for rinsing

Sheets of newsprint for blotting sponge

### BASE COAT

Latex or alkyd satin or eggshell paint

### GLAZE

1 part latex paint

1 part water

*Or commercially prepared glaze*

*We used pale gold for the base; medium gold for the glaze.*

*Before you begin either process, read Basics, pages 7–39.*

*Immediately submerge oil- or solvent-soiled rags in water. Discard according to local ordinances.*

### For Sponging Off
### ADDITIONAL TOOLS

Roller handle

9" roller sleeve with handle

2" foam paintbrush

Rags

Bucket of thinner for rinsing

### BASE COAT

Alkyd or latex semigloss paint

### GLAZE

1 part alkyd paint

1 part alkyd glazing liquid

1 part paint thinner or mineral spirits

Small amount of linseed oil

*We used bisque for the base; taupe for the glaze.*

### TIPS FOR
### SPONGING OFF

• Water-base glazes dry too quickly to be easily sponged off, so we don't recommend them for this technique.

• The color values of the base coat and glaze must be markedly different, or the effect of Sponging Off will not be apparent.

• You'll get better results with two people working side by side: one to roll on the glaze and one to remove it with a sponge. Set aside the time to do an entire wall in one session so that the leading edge will be wet when you paint each adjacent section.

# SPONGING ON

**1** Apply the base coat and let it dry, 2 days for latex, 2–3 days for alkyd.

**2** Mask the walls, ceiling, and baseboard adjacent to where you'll begin. Mix the glaze and pour some of it into the paint tray.

**3** Moisten the sponge with water and wring well. Dip the flat side of the sponge into the glaze in the paint tray, coating the sponge evenly. Squeeze out any excess glaze and blot the sponge on a sheet of paper until you get a neat pattern without smears or blobs.

**4** Starting with a 3' × 3' area, lightly pounce the surface with the sponge, using quick movements of your wrist. Space the dabs approximately 3" apart in a random pattern. Vary the painted print by rotating the sponge each time you lift it.

### TIPS FROM THE PROS

• Be careful not to rotate the sponge on the surface, or the glaze will smear.

• To avoid creating an uneven pattern, reload the sponge whenever the impressions begin to lighten.

• You can fill in the corners as you go or all at once at the end. See Completing Corners, right; also read page 27.

**5** Gradually fill in the spaces until the surface is evenly covered. You should not be able to see where one impression leaves off and another begins. Leave the leading edge of the section irregular so that you can join the adjacent section.

**6** Reload the sponge and repeat with the next section.

### COMPLETING CORNERS

1. Mask one wall in a corner.

2. Tear off a small piece of sponge. Load with glaze and dab the glaze into the corner. Remove the tape.

3. Repeat at each subsequent corner. When the paint is dry, repeat these steps to sponge the other wall in each corner.

**7** Note how the completed surface is evenly sponged, with no open areas of base coat showing through.

• For added depth, use several tones of the same color. Begin sponging with the darkest shade and finish with the lightest shade. Be sure to allow each coat to dry thoroughly before applying the next coat. Shown are two values of yellow over a light yellow base; a third glaze made with the base color was sponged on top of the other colors.

## VARIATIONS

• For a dramatic effect, sponge a light glaze over a dark surface— the sponged paint will seem to float off the wall. Shown here is an off-white glaze sponged over a deep yellow base.

• Sponge on three different colors for a livelier effect. Choose colors that have the same basic intensity. Keep in mind that the last color you apply will be the most dominant. Here two values of orange and a deep blue were sponged over a yellow base; a fourth glaze made with the base color was sponged on top of the other colors.

• To soften or tone down a sponged surface, let the glaze dry completely. Then, using a sponge or a foam roller, cover the surface with another layer of glaze and immediately wipe it off with the sponge or roller (see Stippling with a Foam Roller, page 58). Here is the same multicolored wall as above but overglazed with the two oranges, which were applied randomly at the same time with two sponges.

## SPONGING OFF

**1** Apply the base coat and let it dry, 2 days for latex, 2–3 days for alkyd.

**2** Mask the walls, ceiling, and baseboard adjacent to where you will begin. Mix the glaze and pour some of it into the roller tray. Dip the sponge in thinner; wring it out thoroughly.

**3** Using the foam brush, cut the glaze into the corner where you'll begin; also cut in 18" along the ceiling and baseboard. Load the roller with glaze; remove the excess with the curved painter's tool. Roll two roller widths of glaze from top to bottom; reload as needed. Move the roller in a wavy path along the leading edge.

**4** Pounce the sponge on the wet glaze and then blot the sponge on a rag. Repeat, working in 2' × 2' sections and removing the glaze in a loose spiral pattern.

**TIPS FROM THE PROS**

• Don't try to remove the glaze from the corner in one pass when you begin. Instead, work in and out of the corner as an extension of your spirals, scrunching up the sponge so you can dab it into the corner to remove the glaze. Or use a small piece of sponge; see Handling Corners, page 27.

**5** When the sponge stops removing the glaze, rinse it in thinner and wring it out. Because the clean sponge will remove more glaze, resume pouncing in an unobtrusive area, such as toward the baseboard.

**TIPS FROM THE PROS**

• If you rinse the sponge after every few pounces, much more of the base coat will show through. However, to do this successfully, you'll have to work much faster.

**6** Pounce over the same area, rotating the sponge lightly on the wall, removing more of the glaze, and filling in the spiral.

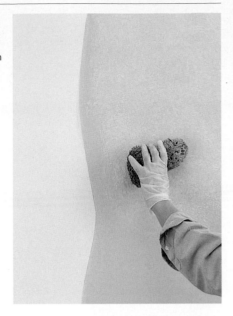

**7** Roll on another ceiling-to-floor swath of glaze and repeat the sponging.

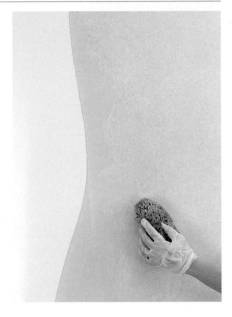

**8** Repeat to complete the wall.

**TIPS FROM THE PROS**

• When you reach the corner, scrunch up the sponge as necessary to remove the glaze (or use a small piece of sponge).

**9** When completed, Sponging Off is much more subtle than Sponging On.

*The effect of Sponging Off falls somewhere between that of Ragging and Stippling, with a haze of color that is slightly crunchy but without the dotted pattern typical of Sponging On. Here emerald green was sponged off a cream wall.*

# SPATTERING

t may make you think of nursery school or modern art, but Spattering is a legitimate and age-old form of decorative painting. It is also an important component of many faux techniques, so even if you don't wish to use it alone, it's a good process to understand. There's nothing mysterious about Spattering. You simply dip a brush into glaze, hold it in front of or above a painted surface, and pull a stick through the bristles to send forth a spray of paint. Keep in mind that the technique is messy and by nature imprecise. On the other hand, the whole family can participate to make the work go quickly.

**TOOLS**
Paint bucket, rack, brushes, and roller for base coat
Pre-taped plastic drop cloth
Latex gloves
Mixing buckets
Stir sticks
Scrap paper or newsprint
Small mixing containers
3" chip brush
Spatter stick (long-handled paintbrush or a stir stick)
Paper towels or rags for cleanup

**BASE COAT**
Latex or alkyd satin paint

**GLAZE**
2 parts latex satin paint
1 part water

Or commercially prepared glaze

*We used dark green for the base; mustard, rose, and deep cherry glazes.*

*Before you begin, read Basics, pages 7–39.*

*Immediately submerge oil- or solvent-soiled rags in water. Discard according to local ordinances.*

*Right: Spattering is a lighthearted choice for a floor—and can camouflage all sorts of worn or inferior materials. Here taupe and two tones of spring green were spattered onto an off-white base. Below: The walls of this cottage guest room have a misty, watery aura. The base coat fades casually from blue below to white above, and spatters of turquoise, blue, and plum add a seaside haze.*

# SPATTERING

**1** Apply the base coat and let it dry, 2 days for latex, 2–3 days for alkyd.

**2** Using the pre-taped plastic drop cloth, mask the ceiling, baseboard, floor, and walls adjacent to where you'll be working. Mix one or more colors of glaze, each in a small container. The glazes should have the consistency of heavy cream.

**TIPS FROM THE PROS**

• If you are spattering a floor, the glaze can be thinner because it won't drip the way it will on a wall. A thinner glaze will spatter in larger flecks.

**3** Test the spattering process: Place some scrap paper or newsprint on the floor or a worktable. Dip the chip brush into the glaze. Hold the brush about 18" above the paper; a narrow side of the brush should face you. Place the handle of the spatter stick on the far side of the loaded brush, perpendicular to it.  Pull the spatter stick toward you across the bristle tips, releasing a spray of paint flecks onto the paper.

**TIPS FROM THE PROS**

• It doesn't matter which hand holds the brush and which the stick. Spattering is less tiring if you swap from time to time.

• The spatter pattern should be fairly light; when you spatter your wall or floor, you can go over an area several times to achieve the desired density. Repeat this test spatter until you find a comfortable distance at which to hold the brush above the paper.

• For larger dots, stand farther away from the wall. For smaller dots, stand closer.

• Once you find a position that gives you the size dots you want, always keep that same distance from the surface.

• If you plan to spatter a floor, you can create a pattern with larger paint flecks by tapping the handle of the loaded brush against the spatter stick (or vice versa). However, large flecks are likely to drip on a wall.

**4** Reload the brush and remove the excess paint by spattering over the paper again.

**TIPS FROM THE PROS**

• Use this process to remove excess paint from the brush every time you reload it.

**5** Hold the loaded brush upright, still in your left hand, so that the narrow edge is parallel to the wall; the brush should be about the same distance from the wall as it was from the paper and fairly close to the ceiling. As before, pull the spatter stick toward you across the bristles, releasing a spray of paint 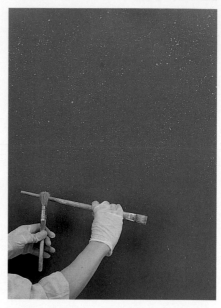 flecks onto the wall. Reposition the brush to the left, right, or below and repeat.

**TIPS FROM THE PROS**

• Don't worry if some of the flecks drip slightly. Small drips are inevitable and add liveliness to the overall effect.

• Pronounced drips can be removed promptly with a damp paper towel. Wrap the towel around your finger, place it at the lower edge of the drip, and slide it upward; then lift your finger away from the wall.

**6** Repeat with the adjacent area. Reload your brush when flecks become too small. Repeat to spatter the remainder of the surface.

**TIPS FROM THE PROS**

• Reposition yourself and the brush frequently as you work. Stand back to view the effect, then repeat the spattering until you get the look you want.

• If you'll be using more than one color glaze, don't make the first pass too dense; you can add more of the same color later.

• You don't have to spatter the entire wall with the first color before adding other colors, but you should complete a ceiling-to-floor area. Be sure the spatters are dry to the touch before you add another color.

**7** Repeat the process with the second color glaze.

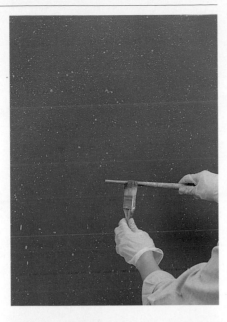

**8** Repeat the process with the third color glaze.

**9** If you wish, spatter on more of any or all of the glazes.

**10** In this sample, the three glazes were applied with equal density. For a different effect, use more of one color than the others.

## VARIATION

• Color choice has everything to do with the impact of a technique like Spattering. Here the same glaze colors used on the green wall above were spattered over an off-white base. The effect is much lighter and airier.

# DRAGGING

**A**lso known as strié, Dragging was popular in the 18th century. Dragged walls generally appear formal; depending on the colors you choose, you can achieve effects that range from subtle and elegant to bright and spirited.

In this technique you apply glaze to a painted surface using a roller, and then, while the glaze is still wet, you drag a brush straight down through it to create fine striations. One caveat: This is a technique that requires a steady hand, speed, practice, and at least one other person to help. And if you're tall enough to easily reach the ceiling with your brush when standing on a step stool, you're in luck—you'll find it easier to drag the glaze in an unbroken line from the ceiling to the baseboard.

*Right: A midnight blue glaze, one layer dragged horizontally and a second layer dragged vertically, throws the grand white moldings in this living room into prominence.*
*Below: Dressy yet not domineering, this pale green dragged wall sets off a collection of antique plates.*
*Bottom: Two layers of mossy green glaze were applied to this wall—the first dragged vertically, the second with informal horizontal curves. Note the door, which was dragged and spattered in a simple country wood grain.*

## TOOLS

Paint bucket, rack, brushes, and roller for base coat

String and washer plumb bobs (see Basics, page 12)

Step stool

3" brown paper painter's tape

Latex gloves

Mixing bucket

Stir stick

Paint tray with tray liner

9" low-nap roller with handle

Curved painter's tool

2" foam brush

Two 3" house painter's brushes

Paper towels or rags for cleanup

## BASE COAT

Latex or alkyd satin paint

## GLAZE

1 part alkyd paint

1 part glazing liquid

2 parts paint thinner or mineral spirits

Small amount of linseed oil

*Or commercially prepared glaze or Latex or Acrylic Glaze (page 16)*

*We used* pale yellow for the base; golden yellow for the glaze.

*Before you begin, read Basics, pages 7–39.*

*Immediately submerge oil- or solvent-soiled rags in water. Discard according to local ordinances.*

## TIPS FOR DRAGGING

• Practice with the color glaze you plan to use to be sure the consistency is right. You can thin the glaze with glazing liquid, which will extend it but keep it thick, or with mineral spirits or water as appropriate, which will dilute it.

• You'll get better results with two people working side by side: one to roll on the glaze and one to drag the brush through it. Set aside the time to do an entire wall in one session so that the leading edge will be wet when you paint each adjacent section.

# DRAGGING

**1** Apply the base coat and let it dry, 2 days for latex, 2–3 days for alkyd.

**2** Mask the walls, ceiling, and baseboard adjacent to where you'll be working. Tape the plumb bobs to the ceiling a couple of inches in front of the wall you'll be painting, spacing them at 2' intervals. Mix the glaze; it should have the consistency of heavy cream. Pour some of the glaze into the paint tray.

**3** Using the foam brush, cut the glaze into the corner where you'll begin; also cut in 18" along the ceiling and baseboard. Load the roller with glaze; remove the excess with the curved painter's tool. Roll two roller widths of glaze from top to bottom; reload as needed.

**4** Starting at the top corner, place the tip of the paintbrush on the wall just below the ceiling. Pressing the ferrule toward the wall and extending your arm out straight, drag the brush down to the baseboard in one continuous stroke. Wipe the brush on a rag. Drag a second band adjacent and parallel to the first.

**5** Repeat as needed to drag the rest of the applied glaze; be sure to leave a 2"-wide wet edge. Redrag the same area, removing as much glaze as needed to create a fine striated pattern. For a lighter effect, you can drag your brush over the same area 3 or 4 times.

**6** Cut in another 18" section along the ceiling and baseboard adjacent to the first section. Roll two roller widths of glaze from top to bottom, reloading as needed. Drag, using the plumb bob as a guide to keep your brush moving in a straight line down the wall.

**7** Redrag as before. Then repeat to complete the wall.

**8** The brush strokes leave very fine and subtle stripes of color that make the finished wall interesting but not busy.

## DRAGGING WOODWORK

• You can also drag woodwork. To do so, apply the glaze with a brush. Using a clean brush, drag off the glaze until you get the desired effect. You can see examples of dragged woodwork in photos on pages 38, 77, and 170.

• For a look that imitates silk shantung, drag a synthetic stripping pad over the glaze. (These squarish pads have a handle centered on one side and are often sold as floor scrubs. You can also use steel wool, but it is harder to hold and the pads disintegrate quickly.)

• For a varied stripe effect, use a chip brush—an inexpensive bristle brush found in most paint stores. Cut the tips off some sections of the bristles to create a more pronounced striation.

• To create a linenlike pattern, apply a second layer of glaze and drag perpendicular to the first striations. To do this, first let the vertically dragged wall dry completely. Apply two roller widths of the second layer of glaze vertically from ceiling to baseboard, as before. Then, beginning in the corner at the ceiling, drag the brush horizontally to the wet edge of the glaze; drag horizontally again immediately below this. Continue in this manner until you reach the baseboard. Apply the next vertical section of glaze, overlapping the dragged area, then continue the horizontal dragging, starting halfway into the previously dragged section.

# STRIPING

**A**dd stripes to a wall when you want to give a tailored look to your decor. Stripes are easy to paint, and while plain contrasting colors are always handsome, you can incorporate virtually any other painting technique into a striped pattern. Once you've planned and marked the repeat on your base-coat-painted surface, you simply tape off alternate sections, apply a contrasting glaze to the exposed portions, and manipulate the glaze if desired. Depending on the colors and paint method you choose, you can make a bold statement or give your walls a subtle elegance. To give you some ideas, we demonstrate ragged stripes and show a couple of variations.

*Right: Cheesecloth-stippled buttery stripes make a pleasing backdrop in this thoughtfully decorative room, complementing the translucent striped shades, stenciled floor border and desk, and printed cushions.*
*Below: These creamy pale and medium yellow stripes were first painted, then mellowed with a yellow glaze rubbed lightly all over.*
*Bottom: In this bold contemporary interior, graphic blue and peach stripes draw the eye to the exposed framing and projecting fireplace.*

## TOOLS

Paint bucket, rack, brushes, and roller for base coat
Chalk line
3" brown paper painter's tape
Latex gloves
Mixing bucket
Stir sticks
Paint tray with tray liner
Foam hot-dog roller with handle
Curved painter's tool
Paper towels (or applicator for chosen painting technique)
Touch-up brush
Paper towels or rags for cleanup

## BASE COAT

Latex or alkyd eggshell or satin paint

## GLAZE

1 part alkyd paint
1 part alkyd glazing liquid
1 part paint thinner or mineral spirits
Small amount of linseed oil

*Or commercially prepared glaze or Latex or Acrylic Glaze (page 16)*

*We used buff for the base; taupe for the glaze.*

*Before you begin, read Basics, pages 7–39, and Stripes and Grids, pages 84–85. Also read the directions for Classic Ragging, pages 59–61. Or if you wish to use another technique, select it and read the directions for it; make any necessary notes for adapting the technique to stripes.*

*Immediately submerge oil- or solvent-soiled rags in water. Discard according to local ordinances.*

# STRIPING

**1** Apply the base coat and let it dry, 2 days for latex, 2–3 days for alkyd.

**2** Measure the width of each wall and determine the width of the stripes (see Stripes and Grids, pages 84–85).

**TIPS FROM THE PROS**

• In general, most spaces will look best with stripes that are 3"–5" wide. The stripes making up the repeat need not be of equal widths.

**3** Mask the ceiling, baseboard, and walls adjacent to the starting wall. Set up chalk guidelines for the stripes, centering them appropriately. Mask the stripes that won't be painted, placing the tape right next to the chalk lines. Tape the entire wall, then wipe off the chalk lines with a clean paper towel.

**4** Mix the glaze; it should have the consistency of heavy cream. Pour some of the glaze into the paint tray. Tear off about 10 five-towel lengths of paper towels. Wad up one length of paper towel to be your first "rag" and keep the others nearby.

**5** Using the hot-dog roller and working from top to bottom, apply the glaze to one stripe. Starting at the top, pounce the rag on the wet glaze, using quick movements of your wrist. Gradually work your way down the stripe.

**TIPS FROM THE PROS**

• You can continue to rag the glazed area until you get the look you desire. The more you pounce, the softer the effect will be.

**6** Promptly remove the tape from each side of the painted stripe. If there's been any seepage under the tape, use a touch-up brush dipped in a little bit of thinner to remove the excess glaze.

**7** Continue to paint the remaining stripes one at a time. Be sure to remove the tape from each and touch up immediately.

**8** Because the colors chosen here are related, the completed wall is interesting yet not overly lively. If you choose colors with more contrast, the effect will be more dramatic.

## STRIPING IDEAS

• There are many ways to approach Striping. A couple of examples follow. Another option is to paint an entire wall with your chosen technique and then overglaze the stripes. And, of course, you can simply paint the stripes in a contrasting color, or for a very subtle effect, use a combination of low- and high-luster paint in the same color.

## VARIATIONS

• Here we spattered the stripes with taupe, and then, after removing all the tape, we spattered all over with white. The final effect is formal without being too serious. Refer to Spattering, pages 72–75, to see how other color combinations might look.

• Though the colors are the same, these stripes, which have been dragged with a synthetic floor scrub, are more subtle than the ragged ones demonstrated on the opposite page. See page 79.

*Playful painting provides a pulled-together look for this old-fashioned bathroom. Sponged-off diamonds embellish the dado. The more open effect on the stripes was achieved by sponging off the alkyd glaze with a sponge dipped first in paint thinner.*

## TRICKS OF THE TRADE
# STRIPES AND GRIDS

If you decide to paint stripes or any pattern calling for a grid configuration (such as faux tiles or a checkerboard), you must plan the proportions of the pattern and mark it on your surface before you begin to paint. Though this preliminary stage may seem tedious or time-consuming, it's important that you think these patterns through to ensure that corners, differing wall proportions, architectural elements such as windows, and any oddities such as sloping floors are accommodated ahead of time. The following assumes you are painting a wall; you can easily adapt the directions to prepare a floor or other surface.

## GETTING STARTED

To begin, ask yourself some questions. You might not have the final answers to the following until you've completed your planning, but you can't get started without a design concept.

• What is the scale of the pattern? For instance, how wide is the stripe or how large is the tile, and is it square or rectangular?

• Will your pattern be regular or irregular? Will the stripes have equal or unequal widths? Will alternate rows of tiles or blocks be aligned or staggered?

• Do you want the pattern centered on the surface? For instance, should the center of a stripe or tile be placed on the vertical center of the wall, or should two stripes or a tile grout line be on the vertical center? Either way can be fine, but depending upon the proportions of the pattern and the wall, one might be more pleasing than the other or might work better at corners.

• Is the pattern going on adjacent walls? Is it important that the pattern repeat be complete on the wall, or can it continue around corners? If the pattern repeat should be complete, refer to Repeating Patterns, pages 96–97.

• If you are painting a grid pattern, will there be grout lines, for instance, between tiles or stone blocks? How wide?

• Will the pattern cover the entire surface or only a portion of it? If you are painting a dado, how will you paint the top edge?

Once you've answered these questions, you can mark the pattern on the wall. If you are uncertain about the spacing of the pattern on the wall, make a scale drawing on graph paper first.

First, find and mark the vertical center of your wall. Measure from each corner at the ceiling, floor, and at several points in between. Snap a chalk line from ceiling to floor (see opposite page). Use a spirit level to check that the line is plumb. If it is not, adjust the marks, brush off the first line, and snap again.

**TIPS FROM THE PROS**

• Most stripe patterns can continue around corners. If you prefer, center them on each wall and let the corner stripes fall as they may.

• Tile and block patterns look best centered on each wall; they should be cut at corners, regardless of whether the repeat is complete.

• Most block and tile patterns look best when the bottom course is a full unit deep. If a vertical repeat is such that a very shallow incomplete unit falls below the ceiling, adjust the unit size or make the bottom course deeper than the others. However, if you are painting a dado, the course immediately below the top "trim" should be the full unit depth.

## PREPARING STRIPES

Determine the width of your stripes. Measure and mark the appropriate intervals on the wall with a pencil or blackboard chalk; mark at the ceiling, floor, and several places in between.

• If you wish to center a stripe on the wall, measure and mark half the stripe width on each side of the center chalk line. Then measure the full stripe width away from these marks, marking each interval.

• If you wish to place one stripe on each side of the center chalk line, measure the stripe width away from the center chalk line, marking each interval. Snap a vertical chalk line to connect each set of marks.

Mask the stripes that won't be painted, positioning the tape so that the chalk line is exposed on each edge of the stripe that is to be painted.

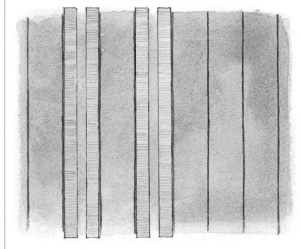

**TIPS FROM THE PROS**

• If you continue a stripe around a corner, check that the first line you snap is plumb and adjust it if necessary.

## SNAPPING A CHALK LINE

Chalk lines, available in paint and hardware stores, are small boxes containing 50'–100' of string on a reel and, in many cases, blue chalk. Because the blue chalk is difficult to wipe off, you should empty out the box and refill it with a mixture of 3 parts talcum powder and 1 part blue chalk.

To snap a chalk line longer than 3' you'll need a partner. One person should hold the chalk box on the mark at one edge of the surface while the other stretches the string to the mark at the opposite edge and holds it taut. One person should reach toward the center, position the taut string against one of the marks, and then lift the string away from the surface and release it. It will leave a straight, powdery line between the marks.

### TIPS FROM THE PROS
- Use three people to snap long lines; each should hold the string with one hand against a measured mark and then snap it with the other hand.
- Paint and glaze won't adhere to chalk. Once you've masked the pattern, brush or wipe off the chalk (use a clean paper towel).
- You can't erase pencil marks that have been painted over. If your paint or glaze is not opaque, erase the marks before painting.

## PREPARING GRIDS

Determine the size of your grid unit. If your pattern features grout lines, include the grout width in each dimension. For instance, if you want to create 12" square tiles with $^1/_4$" grout lines, the grid unit must be $12^1/_4$" square. Read the following all the way through before beginning.

Measure, mark, and snap the horizontal lines onto your wall.
- If your grid extends from floor to ceiling, measure and mark the height of one unit above the baseboard all across the wall. Snap a horizontal chalk line and use a spirit level to check that it is level. Measuring up from this line, snap the subsequent horizontal lines onto the wall.
- If your grid extends only partway up the wall, position and snap the top line first, check that it is level, and then measure from the top down to snap the subsequent lines.

Measure, mark, and snap the vertical intervals onto the wall.
- If your grid is regular, measure, mark, and snap the vertical lines as for stripes (see opposite page).

- If your grid is staggered, mark and snap the vertical intervals. Then very lightly pencil in the lines on alternate horizontal courses. Brush off the vertical chalk lines. Mark and snap another set of vertical lines, spacing them equally between the first set. Lightly pencil in these lines on the horizontal courses not marked previously.

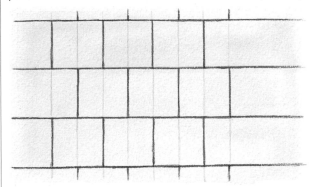

Mask the grid to prepare for painting.
- If you are painting a checkerboard, mask all the edges of alternate squares, positioning the tape inside the squares not to be painted and leaving the chalk lines exposed. Cut the tape so that it fits neatly in each square.
- If your grid unit includes grout lines, apply narrow masking tape to the top and right edges of each unit. Note that this means the center of the painted unit will not be the same as the center of the measured unit. If this will bother you, the first vertical line you snap in the center of your wall should be off center, to the right, by half the grout width.

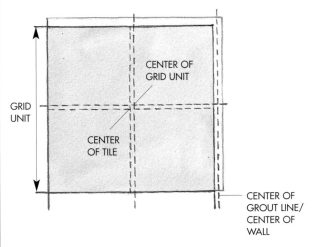

### TIPS FROM THE PROS
- You can purchase narrow tape in widths of $^1/_{16}$"–$^1/_4$" at a good office or art supply store. Computer graphics have largely replaced the narrower widths, so you might have to ask your vendor to order them for you. If you are painting a large area, be aware that the tape can be expensive.
- Apply the tape consistently to the top and right edges of each unit. If you switch edges, the painted units will vary in size.

Combing is often associated with country decor, but it can be quite sophisticated and either bold or delicate, depending upon the comb, colors, and pattern used. There are many different combing tools in various widths and with different size teeth; when dragged through wet glaze, each produces a pattern in a different scale. You can also make combs from plastic lids or cardboard, but cardboard wears out quickly and so is not recommended for large areas. Combing can be effective on floors, doors, and woodwork, as well as on walls. Here we give directions for three patterns—Straight Combing, Basketweave, and Moiré. Follow them as shown or experiment to create your own.

*Right: In a contemporary interpretation of this technique, a wide-toothed comb—perhaps cut from a plastic lid—was pulled horizontally and then, while the glaze was still wet, vertically, creating a simple allover pattern. Below: A pattern of random arcs and shallow curves offers another combing option for a contemporary interior. Bottom: Short strokes of a cardboard comb through a vinegar glaze (page 112) gave a country finish to these kitchen cabinets.*

## TOOLS

Paint bucket, rack, brushes, and roller for base coat

Step stool

3" brown paper painter's tape

String and washer plumb bobs (see Basics, page 12)

Mixing bucket

Latex gloves

Stir sticks

Paint tray with tray liner

Hot-dog foam roller with handle

Curved painter's tool

2" foam brush

Two 3" house painter's brushes

Triangular rubber graining comb (for straight and basketweave patterns)

9" graining comb (for moiré combing)

Paper towels or rags for cleanup

## BASE COAT

Latex or alkyd satin paint

## GLAZE

1 part alkyd paint

1 part alkyd glazing liquid

1 part paint thinner or mineral spirits

Small amount of linseed oil

*Or commercially prepared glaze or Latex or Acrylic Glaze (page 16)*

We used off-white for the base; medium sky blue for the glaze.

*Before you begin, read Basics, pages 7–39. Read the directions all the way through and decide what kind of combing pattern and tool to use.*

*Immediately submerge oil- or solvent-soiled rags in water. Discard according to local ordinances.*

## TIPS FOR COMBING

• Test the pattern on a wall before beginning (refer to Basics, page 20). You'll become comfortable with the tool, see how much pressure is needed, and be able to judge whether the pattern is the right scale for the room.

• You'll have better results with two people working side by side: one to roll on the glaze and one to drag and then comb it. Set aside the time to do an entire wall in one session so that the leading edge will be wet when you paint the adjacent section.

# STRAIGHT COMBING

**1** Apply the base coat and let it dry, 2 days for latex, 2–3 days for alkyd.

**2** Mask the walls, ceilings, and baseboard adjacent to where you'll be working. Hang plumb bobs a couple of inches in front of the wall, about 2' apart. Mix the glaze; it should have the consistency of heavy cream. Pour some of the glaze into the paint tray.

**3** Using the foam brush, cut the glaze into the corner where you'll begin; also cut in 18" along the ceiling and baseboard. Load the roller with glaze; remove the excess with the curved painter's tool. Roll two roller widths of glaze from top to bottom; reload as needed. Be sure to roll the glaze evenly.

**4** Starting at the corner, place the tip of the paintbrush on the wall just below the ceiling. Pressing the ferrule toward the wall and extending your arm out straight, drag the brush down to the baseboard in one continuous stroke. Drag a second band adjacent and parallel to the first. Repeat as needed to drag the rest of the applied glaze; be sure to leave a 2"-wide wet edge. Redrag the same area until the glaze is no longer runny.

## TIPS FROM THE PROS

• Clean your brush as needed by wiping on a rag. When the rag no longer cleans the glaze off that brush, switch to the second brush.

**5** Select your combing tool; we used a rubber graining tool with graduated teeth. Starting at the top corner of the area you just dragged, hold the comb parallel to the ceiling, press the teeth against the wall, and pull the comb straight down to the baseboard. Clean the comb with a rag. Starting directly next to the area you just completed, comb the adjacent section; do not overlap the pattern.

## TIPS FROM THE PROS

• Avoid lifting the comb partway down the wall, or you'll interrupt the pattern.

• If you turn the graduated comb over every time you reposition it at the ceiling, the wide and narrow stripes will alternate in wider bands. Be consistent or not, as you wish.

**6** Continue as needed until you've combed all of the dragged glaze; be sure to clean the comb after each pass.

**7** Cut in another 18" section along the ceiling and baseboard adjacent to the first section. Roll two roller widths of glaze from top to bottom, reloading as needed. Repeat the combing process. Continue in this manner to comb the entire wall.

## COMPLETING CORNERS

• If when you get to the end of the wall you're combing, your last width is less than the width of your combing tool, cut a comb to fit from a plastic lid, cutting V-shaped notches in one straight side.

**8** At first glance the completed combing appears perfect, but of course it was done freehand and the lines are not absolutely straight. Note that you can't see any demarcation lines and that the color is even.

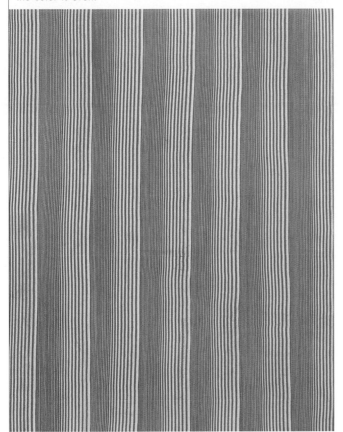

**VARIATION**

• If you are using a graduated graining tool, you can create an informal plaid by combing horizontally over the vertically combed surface while the glaze is still wet. Comb one section of applied glaze at a time, as explained opposite, carrying the horizontal combing just beyond the wet edge. Then apply the next section of glaze, overlapping the first, and repeat the vertical and then the horizontal combing. Continue in this fashion until you complete the surface.

**TIPS FROM THE PROS**

• Take care not to turn the graduated graining tool over when you reposition it. Once you've set up the horizontal pattern, always align the teeth with the established pattern before combing into the new glaze.

# BASKETWEAVE COMBING

**1** Follow steps 1–4 for Straight Combing.

**2** Select your combing tool; we used the fine-toothed side of a triangular graining tool. Starting at the top corner and working down, vertically comb a section as deep as your comb is wide, forming a square. Hold the comb perpendicular and adjacent to the first combed square 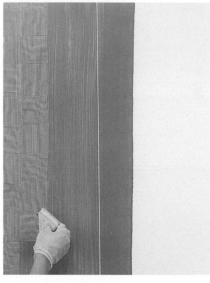 and comb another square the same width. Continue to comb, alternating vertical and horizontal squares from top to bottom.

### TIPS FROM THE PROS

• To make a guide for the depth of the first square, hold the comb at the top of the wall in the corner, with the teeth aligned with the adjacent wall—as if you were about to comb horizontally—and nick the glaze with the lowest tooth. Then reposition the comb with the teeth aligned with the ceiling and pull it vertically to the nick.

**3** When you reach the bottom, begin again at the top and continue in a checkerboard pattern of alternating squares. Do not comb over the previously combed pattern.

### TIPS FROM THE PROS

• To make a guide for the width of the first horizontal square  at the top of the wall, hold the comb adjacent to the previous column of squares, as if you were about to comb vertically, and nick the glaze with the outermost tooth. Then reposition the comb and pull it horizontally to the nick.

**4** Continue in this manner to comb the rest of the applied glaze; do not comb into the leading edge.

**5** Cut in another 18" section along the ceiling and baseboard adjacent to the first section. Roll two roller widths of glaze from top to bottom, reloading as needed. Repeat the combing process.

### TIPS FROM THE PROS

• Before working horizontally in the newly applied glaze, be sure to work all the way from ceiling to baseboard adjacent to the previously combed section.

**6** Continue in this manner to comb the entire wall.

### COMPLETING CORNERS

• If when you get to the end of the wall you're combing, your last width is less than the width of your combing tool, cut a comb to fit from a plastic lid, cutting V-shaped notches in one straight side. Use this for the vertical sections of the basketweave, but continue to use the previously used tool for the horizontal sections.

**7** Because you repeatedly lift and reposition the comb as you work the wet glaze, the density of color in a basketweave pattern is irregular. As with straight combing, it's virtually impossible to make a perfect repeat freehand, and the final effect is full of movement.

# MOIRÉ COMBING

**1** Follow steps 1–4 for Straight Combing. In step 4, begin at the top but hold the paintbrush horizontally and drag it across the wet glaze, stopping just short of the wet edge.

**2** Starting at the top corner of the area you just dragged, hold the comb perpendicular to the ceiling, press the teeth against the wall, and pull the comb horizontally across the glaze. Do not comb the leading edge. Starting directly adjacent to and underneath the first pattern, comb another horizontal pattern. Repeat until you reach the bottom of the wall.

**3** Position the comb at the top corner as before. To create the moiré pattern, comb the same area horizontally again, but this time move the comb up and down in a wavy motion as you go. Stop before you reach the end of the previously combed pattern. Repeat below and parallel to the first wavy pattern. Repeat to comb the rest of the applied glaze.

### TIPS FROM THE PROS

• Be sure to keep the comb perpendicular to the floor while you move it up and down in a wavy pattern. If you tilt the comb the pattern will get out of whack.

• As you comb the wavy pattern, stagger your stopping position. This will minimize demarcation lines that might appear later when you apply and comb into the next section of glaze.

**4** Cut in another 18" section along the ceiling and baseboard adjacent to the first section. Roll two roller widths of glaze from top to bottom, reloading as needed.

**5** Beginning again at the ceiling, align the teeth of the comb in the end of the previous straight combing pattern and pull the comb through the wet glaze, stopping short of the leading edge as before. Then align the teeth in the end of the wavy pattern and continue it across the wet glaze, stopping inside the straight pattern, as before. Repeat to comb the rest of the applied glaze.

**6** Continue in this manner to comb the rest of the wall.

**7** When complete, the moiré pattern really looks like the elegant fabric it mimics. You might think this is one of the more difficult techniques to do well, but in truth the pattern is very forgiving—the effect of overall movement camouflages mistakes.

tamped motifs offer a quick and simple way to add pattern to a painted surface. You can use ready-made or custom rubber stamps, sponge shapes, or fruits and vegetables, as we did. Because the motifs are applied one at a time, there is no wet glaze requiring quick manipulation. So whether you decide upon a random or controlled pattern, you can apply it in stages or let everyone in the family participate at once. The following directions can easily be adapted to apply a design of your choice. For a more sophisticated look, try Stamping over another technique, such as Colorwashing, Rubbing, or Sponging.

*Right: This fanciful wall is embellished with a variously random and controlled pattern of small graphic motifs— stars, half moons, circles, and diamonds— stamped in gold over a sponged, softened green and blue ombré ground. Below: Blue and silver stamped leaves float casually down a pale blue colorwashed wall. Bottom: To stamp a controlled pattern like this, first cut four squares of synthetic sponge and glue them onto a wood block.*

### TOOLS

Paint bucket, rack, brushes, and roller for base coat
Chalk line, ruler, and pencil for marking wall
Potato, fruits, and pencil with unused eraser for stamps (or purchased rubber stamps)
Chef's knife, paring knife, and cutting board
Artist's palette or plastic lids
Latex gloves
Small mixing containers
Mixing brushes
Newsprint
Kneadable eraser
Foam hot-dog roller with handle (optional, for overglaze)
Paper towels or rags for cleanup

### BASE COAT

Latex or alkyd satin paint

### GLAZES

Acrylic stencil paints or artist's acrylics (tube or liquid)
Acrylic matte medium
Acrylic gel retarder (as needed)

Oil Glaze or Latex Glaze (page 16) for optional overglaze

*We used* light aqua for the base coat; medium and deep aqua, medium and deep purple, and acid green for stamping; off-white for the overglaze.

*Before you begin, read Basics, pages 7–39. Also read Stripes and Grids, pages 84–85. Read the following directions all the way through, then test and adapt them as desired.*

*If you use an oil-base final glaze, be sure to immediately submerge used rags in water. Discard according to local ordinances.*

# STAMPING

## STAMPING WITH FRUITS AND VEGETABLES

- The cut surface of various fruits and vegetables holds glaze in different ways, so some are easier to use as stamps than others. Experiment before you commit to a design.
- For best results, once you have chosen the stamps that make an image you like, test each on a painted wall, not on paper, to see how hard you have to press and how much paint to use. Do this before you apply the base coat to the wall so that you can paint out the test.
- The cut surface of the stamps should be as flat and smooth as possible.
- Some fruits or vegetables will work best if you brush the paint onto them; others will work fine if you just press them into the paint on the artist's palette.

**1** Apply the base coat and let it dry, 2 days for latex, 2–3 days for alkyd.

**2** If you wish to use a repeating pattern, plan it and mark appropriate guidelines on your wall. (We used a 7½" grid.) To prepare for the 9-patch square pattern (three rows of three small squares), we lightly marked an X from corner to corner of alternate squares on the grid.

**3** To make a potato stamp, first cut a potato in half. Draw the shape you want on newsprint and cut it out. (We used a 1½" square.) Lay the cutout on the cut side of the potato. With the paring knife, cut away the potato around the newsprint, leaving a raised pattern about ½" high.

### TIPS FROM THE PROS
- If you want your potato motif to appear in more than one color, make a stamp for each color.

**4** Prepare each color glaze in a separate small container. If you are using stencil paints, mix 4 parts paint and 1 part medium. If you are using artist's tube acrylics, first mix 2 parts paint with 1 part water, then mix 4 parts of this with 1 part medium; if you are using liquid acrylics, you may not need as much water. The glazes should be quite thick, with the consistency of pudding. You can thin them further when you work with them if necessary.

**5** Pour some of the first color glaze onto the palette. Also put some retarder on the palette. Using the mixing brush, spread the glaze and mix in a little retarder. Brush some of the glaze onto the potato stamp.

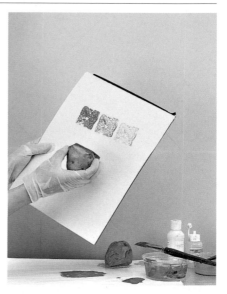

**6** Test the design on a piece of newsprint. If the result is not to your liking, try dipping the stamp into the glaze or making the glaze thicker or thinner by adding more paint or more medium to the mixture on the palette. Experiment until you get the look you desire.

**7** Press the stamp on the wall in the center of one marked square (each corner of the stamp should sit on an arm of the X). Leaving a space of about ½", press another square next to the first. Continue stamping until you finish a 9-patch pattern. Change to another color at any time, testing it as before. Continue, making a checkerboard of 9-patch patterns.

- The 9-patch pattern shown is truly random. To create it, two people each stamped a different color, moving around the wall and making a few stamps in one part of the grid, a few more in another part.
- This technique is best for creating an informal pattern. Don't worry if the stamped motifs are irregular or vary in paint coverage.
- You don't have to complete the checkerboard before adding other motifs.
- If the glaze begins to dry on the palette, blend in a bit of the retarder.

**8** Select apples, pears, or other fruits to use as stamp motifs. Those that are asymmetrical or somewhat eccentric will be more interesting. Cut the fruits in half, lengthwise or crosswise as you wish, and wrap them in plastic wrap until ready to use. (They'll keep in the refrigerator for about a week.)

**TIPS FROM THE PROS**

- After cutting, remove any seeds—the remaining holes will enhance the design.
- If you can, cut stems in half too. If they don't automatically print on the wall, press them against it with a finger.

**9** Place additional colors of glaze on a palette as before. Coat the cut side of a fruit with glaze and press it onto the wall to alternate with the 9-patch pattern. Do the same with a different fruit and different color glaze. Continue, making your pattern as colorful as you wish.

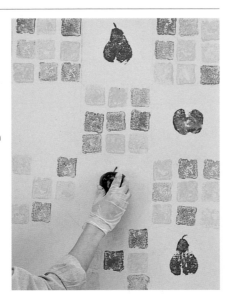

**10** Cut the star fruit in half crosswise. Press the cut side into the desired glaze and press it onto the wall in random spaces to fill in the design. Superimpose some of the star prints on some of the squares.

**11** Press the end of the pencil eraser into one color glaze. Press it onto the wall at the corners of the checkerboard. Clean the eraser and change colors frequently, making 4 dots at each corner.

**12** When the glaze is dry, remove any remaining pencil guides with the kneadable eraser. If you wish, apply an overglaze to soften the pattern, following the directions for Stippling with a Foam Roller on page 58 or Rubbing Off on page 54.

**13** This stamped pattern is reminiscent of 1950s linoleum, but of course you can set up any pattern you like. One as dense as this would be great above or below a chair rail or as a backsplash.

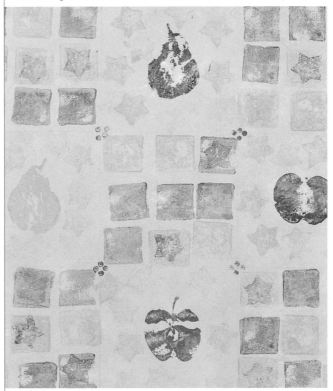

A repeating pattern is any design with a graphic motif that is evenly spaced on a background. Stripes and checkerboards are simple repeating patterns; stencils are usually more complex. The motif can be contiguous (touching), as in the Border Stencil on pages 102–103, or discrete (spaced apart), or a combination, as in the Damask Stencil design on pages 100–101.

Getting a repeating pattern to fit neatly in a given space is a mathematical exercise, almost always combined with a little trial and error. Don't expect to get it right on the first try. Experienced designers may have better luck judging the relative sizes of the repeat and the wall, but even they have to make sure the pattern fits attractively and decide how to adjust it if necessary.

## SIZING THE REPEAT

First determine the size of the repeat. If you are working with a motif that is already set up to be contiguous, for instance, a unit on a grid or a border, just measure it. If your motif is discrete, you'll have to decide how much space you want between the repeating motifs and incorporate that into your measurement, effectively turning it into a unit you can place on a grid.

### FOR STRIPES

Stripes have only one dimension to measure—the width, which can repeat horizontally or vertically, depending upon the way the stripe is placed on the wall. A horizontal stripe creates a vertical repeat, a vertical stripe creates a horizontal repeat. It takes two or more bars of color to make a striped pattern; be sure to include one of each bar when you measure the repeat.

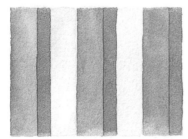

### TIPS FROM THE PROS

• The center of a stripe and the center of a stripe repeat are not the same. You can position either one at the center of the wall.

### FOR BORDERS

Borders may look like horizontal or vertical stripes, but if they are anything more complex than lines of contrasting color paralleling an edge, they are made up of a motif that repeats in one dimension only. A vertical border has a vertical repeat; a horizontal border has a horizontal repeat.

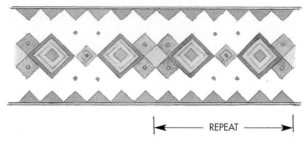

|← REPEAT →|

### TIPS FROM THE PROS

• Of course, the motif creating a border has two dimensions, but only one of these is important for determining the repeat.

### FOR GRIDS

Patterns that fit on grids have both a horizontal and a vertical repeat. To find the horizontal repeat, measure the greatest width of the motif. To find the vertical repeat, measure the greatest length. If your motif is discrete, find these dimensions and add to each an estimated amount for the space you want between repeating motifs. Make a sketch to help you visualize the effect and see how to incorporate the motif on a grid.

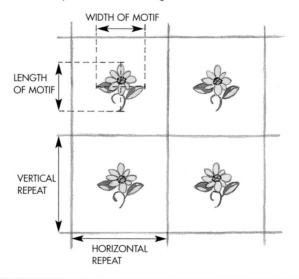

WIDTH OF MOTIF

LENGTH OF MOTIF

VERTICAL REPEAT

HORIZONTAL REPEAT

### TIPS FROM THE PROS

• If you are working with a stencil design, make a test to see how the repeat aligns and then measure the test, measuring from one point on the motif (for instance, the tip of a leaf) to the same point on the next motif. This is more accurate than measuring the stencil itself, which might not include the entire blank space between motifs.

## CHECKING THE REPEAT

To see how a motif will repeat on your wall, do the following.

**For a horizontal repeat,** divide the repeat into the width of the wall. The result is the number of times the motif will fit across the wall, plus any excess.

**For a vertical repeat,** divide the repeat into the height of the wall, excluding any moldings. The result is the number of times the motif will fit between the baseboard and ceiling, plus any excess.

You have several choices to accommodate the excess that almost certainly will appear in your calculations.

• Adjust the size of the motif so that it repeats perfectly. This is easier to do for a stripe than for other patterns. Also, you can adjust the open area around a discrete motif fairly easily, but bear in mind that the grid it sits on will probably become rectangular in order to fit both lengthwise and widthwise on the wall.

• Decide to make some portion or portions of the repeat unequal by allowing just a bit more space between them. Usually the best place to do this is at both ends, though sometimes the center works too. Whatever you decide, make the adjustment symmetrical. Sometimes you can supplement these adjustments by adding or extending a small element from the motif, such as a flourish, leaf, bud, or small geometric shape.

## CREATING A DROP REPEAT

A drop repeat is one in which the horizontal alignment of the repeating motif is offset, or dropped, by half the length of the vertical repeat. To understand a drop repeat, visualize your design in columns, and shift alternate columns so that the top of the motif in one column aligns with the horizontal midpoint of the motif in the adjacent column. In other words, begin and end alternate columns with a half vertical repeat, the other columns with a full vertical repeat. The Damask Stencil Variation on page 101 is a drop repeat on a vertical rectangular grid.

## TURNING A CORNER

If you'd like a border or stripe to turn a corner—for instance, to parallel window trim—plan first. Stripes are easy to turn, but repeating motifs can be challenging. Some miter neatly. Motifs that are scalloped or not connected on one long edge can be fanned as they turn; depending upon the design, you may need to supplement the pattern with an extra whole or partial scallop or similar element. Work out the corner, then plan the repeat of the full motif in each direction. If more than one corner is involved and the repeat is not working between them, move the border closer to or farther away from the edge it parallels or add a complementary motif midway between corners.

*This stenciled border makes two turns at the top of the wall to accommodate the stairway. Designs with pendant (hanging) motifs, such as this typical Victorian stylized palm leaf, are especially good choices for turning corners—even if the motif doesn't repeat perfectly, you can usually fan or bend it attractively. Note the simple stripe border with elaborate corner embellishment on the ceiling.*

# STENCILING

Use Stenciling to add graphic pattern to your decor. Precut stencils are available in myriad styles—the options range from traditional Early American to sophisticated to whimsical. If you don't see the perfect design, consider combining some unrelated ones, as we did to create the Two-Color Border. Consider also that unexpected colors can transform a design. There are many stencil paints ready-mixed in a vast range of colors and qualities—from matte to metallic. On the next few pages we show how to stencil using one, two, and multiple colors and motifs.

## TOOLS

Paint bucket, rack, brushes, and roller for base coat

Chalk line, ruler, and pencil or chalk for marking wall

Precut stencil(s)

Masking tape

Adjustable spray adhesive

Artist's palette or large plastic lid

Latex gloves

Small mixing containers

Mixing brush

Stencil brush(es)

Paper towels

Small artist's brushes for touch-up and details

Natural cosmetic sponge for details

Paper towels or rags for cleanup

## BASE COAT

Latex or alkyd eggshell or satin paint

## STENCIL PAINT

Acrylic stencil paints or artist's tube acrylics and Acrylic Medium (page 18)

Acrylic gel retarder (as needed)

If you'd prefer to use oil-base stencil paints, see Stenciling with Oil Paint, page 101.

*For the Damask Stencil we used old rose for the base coat; deep rose for the stenciling.*

*For the Border Stencil we used pale sky blue for the base coat; medium sky blue and white with deep sky blue accents for the stenciling. The outer border was first dragged in medium sky blue glaze.*

*For the Multicolor Stencil we used off-white for the base coat and assorted playful colors for the stenciling.*

*Before you begin, read Basics, pages 7–39. Also read Repeating Patterns, pages 96–97. Read the following directions all the way through before starting to paint.*

*If you use oil-base paints, be sure to immediately submerge used paper towels in water. Discard according to local ordinances.*

## TIPS FOR STENCILING

• Always paint a test of your stencil design before using it on your surface. Be sure you understand the repeat and/or alignment of the motifs. (Many precut stencils have somewhat imperfectly aligned repeats; as long as you are aware of this when you begin, you should be able to compensate as you work.)

*Right: The leaf pattern spilling below this border is a negative stencil—an acetate pattern was glued to the wall, which was then sponged off. When the pattern was removed, hand-painted details were added.*
*Below: A border stenciled on plaster looks like an antique fresco.*
*Bottom: A stencil was used to outline this border. The colors were applied with artist's brushes for a more painterly effect.*

# STENCILING

## PREPARING A STENCIL

• Some stencils come with registration marks, such as a small circle or crossed lines. Sometimes the registration marks consist of the repeated motif outlines. Both types are used to align the design when you reposition the stencil. Often, but not always, you can find the size of the repeat by measuring the distance between the registration marks.

• If you will be painting a complex allover design like the damask motif shown here and motif registration guides are not marked on the stencil, your test stenciling should include a repeat of the motif in each appropriate direction. Paint the test, then clean the stencil, place it over the central test motif, and trace some key portions of the surrounding motifs onto the acetate. You'll find it easier and more accurate to align motifs than small registration marks.

• Mark the horizontal and vertical centers of the motif as well and use them as a guide for planning the position of the stencil on your surface.

• To avoid confusion, put a masking tape label on the side of the stencil that should face you as you paint.

## DAMASK STENCIL

**1** Apply the base coat and let it dry, 2 days for latex, 2–3 days for alkyd.

**2** Figure out your repeating pattern and decide where you will begin to stencil. Mark the starting position on your surface; use a chalk line or a simple chalk or pencil mark, as appropriate.

### KNOWING WHERE TO START

• Generally, you work from top to bottom and from one side of the surface to the other. This makes it less likely that a dropped brush loaded with paint will mar the area you've stenciled. It's easier to clean accidents from an unstenciled area.

• However, for an allover pattern with a tight repeat, such as the one shown, you should start at the center and work out in all directions—this will allow you to compensate for any lack of "square" in the design (or the wall) and avoid having a pattern that runs downhill or has to be overlapped incorrectly.

**3** Lightly spray the back of the stencil with the adhesive and let it set for a few minutes, until tacky. Line up the center of the stencil with the center of the surface and press it into position.

### TIPS FROM THE PROS

• To ensure a tight seal, gently rub the stencil into place with a folded paper towel.

**4** If you are using stencil paint, place a tablespoonful on the artist's palette. If you are using tube acrylics, place a small amount on the palette and blend it with the mixed acrylic medium in a ratio of 2 parts paint to 1 part medium. Lightly dip the stencil brush into the paint. Rub the bristles over a folded paper towel to off-load some of the paint. The brush should leave a light, even paint impression before you apply it to your surface. If a tube paint blend seems too thick, add a little water to it.

**5** Lightly swirl the brush over the stencil. Work from one edge toward the opposite edge. Make the paint density as translucent, opaque, or varied as you like; you can work over an area more than once until you achieve the desired effect. Blend in some retarder if the paint dries too quickly.

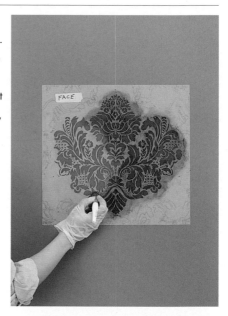

**6** Reload the brush as necessary and complete the first motif. Carefully peel off the stencil. Touch up any seepage. Reposition the stencil, being sure to align the registration marks. Stencil as before.

### TIPS FROM THE PROS

• Be sure the motif just painted is dry before you realign the stencil on top of it.

• If the paint on the stencil obscures the registration marks, wipe it off. If you use a damp sponge or towel, be sure the stencil is dry before you reposition it.

**7** Reposition the stencil again and repeat the painting process.

**8** Continue in this manner until you've stenciled the desired area. Clean the stencil and reapply the adhesive as necessary.

**9** The choice of a traditional motif makes this allover stencil a good stand-in for expensive wallpaper or fabric. Applying such a dense pattern to a large area is time-consuming, so you might want to confine it within a "framed" area or use it to embellish a folding screen or flat doors.

**VARIATION**

• Stencils are often packaged with multiple components, such as companion borders and corner motifs, which offer a variety of design options. Here the allover motif was paired with a corner motif to form a drop repeat above the border "chair rail"—all stenciled over a ragged wall. This arrangement takes some planning but can be stenciled in much less time than the allover repeat.

**STENCILING WITH OIL PAINT**
• Oil-base stenciling is more durable than water-base, but since stenciling is a technique in which you want the paint to dry quickly, artist's oils are not a good paint choice. Should you wish to stencil with oil paint, use japan colors, which dry quickly; they are available at art supply stores. Mix 2 parts of japan color with 1 part mineral spirits or thinner. Test the paint following steps 4 and 5, opposite. If necessary, adjust the consistency of the mixture.

# TWO-COLOR BORDER STENCIL

**1** Prepare your stencils (see page 100). Stencil a test of your design and make sure the colors read clearly and cleanly—especially if one color is applied on top of another.

**TIPS FROM THE PROS**

• If you are using only a portion of the stencil motif—as we did to add the birds and flowers to our border—decide how much you'll use and mask the unwanted portion.

• The motifs on our second stencil were cut so close to the edge that paint strayed over the edge onto our test. So we used a larger piece of acetate to extend the stencil background as well as mask the design. We simply cut an opening in this supplementary piece to expose the motifs we wanted, and taped the two layers together.

**2** Read the complete directions for Damask Stencil, pages 100–101. Referring to your test, complete steps 1–8, using the first stencil and the first color only. Begin at the top and work down. Note that the design shown here ends with a half repeat at the corner.

**TURNING CORNERS**

• Some border stencils are designed to turn corners. Others, especially loose designs like the one shown here, can be adapted to do so. But be alert—some designs have motifs that work in only one orientation.

• Plan the corner alignment on paper—tracing paper or a photocopier can help—and then mark appropriate corner guidelines onto the surface you're stenciling.

• Measure out from the marked guidelines to make sure the motif repeats successfully between corners. If it doesn't, you'll have to increase or decrease the distance between the border and the edge it parallels.

• If you have any doubts, before you paint, align the stencil with the corner guidelines on your surface and mark the end of the first repeat with chalk. Reposition the stencil and mark the end of the next repeat. Continue until you've marked all the repeats.

**3** If you are turning a corner, reposition the stencil as planned. Here we needed only a portion of the motif when we rotated the stencil, so we masked the unwanted areas with tape. Continue to stencil.

**4** Complete the stenciling of the first color according to your plan. Remove and reapply any masking as needed.

**5** Referring to your test, align the second stencil over the painted border. Apply the second color through the stencil. Reposition the second stencil and repeat. Here we sometimes added both the bird and flower and sometimes just the flower, in which case we masked the bird with tape.

**6** Complete the stenciling of the second color according to your plan. Remove and reapply any masking as needed.

**7** If you wish, use an artist's brush to add freehand details to your design.

### TIPS FROM THE PROS

• To add delicate streaks to elements such as flower petals, stroke the brush from the base of the streak toward the tip—in this case away from the flower center. Surprisingly, an old brush with frayed bristles is the perfect tool.

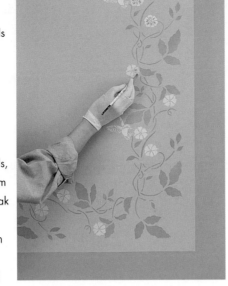

**8** Use borders to accent architectural details such as door or window moldings or to stand in for chair rails or crown moldings where none exist. Here we dragged a frame before adding the border; if you use this approach to make a rectangular border on a plain wall, you'll create a decorative panel.

*This wonderfully complex ceiling began with a base coat of off-white, gradually embellished with sponging, then stenciling, then more sponging. The border design is actually a negative stencil—the dark background paint was applied through the stencil, creating the lighter scrolled leaf pattern.*

# MULTICOLOR STENCIL

**1** Prepare your stencils (see page 100). Stencil a test of your design and make sure the colors read clearly and cleanly—especially if one color is applied on top of another.

**2** Read the directions for Damask Stencil and Two-Color Border Stencil, pages 100–101 and 102–103. We've chosen to stencil a single repeat of a complex design for which registration is required for positioning the individual motifs. If you will be painting a repeating design, check the overall repeat and plan to apply the first color to all the repeats, then the second color, and so on, as described in the Two-Color Border Stencil directions.

**3** Complete steps 1–5 of Damask Stencil, stenciling the first motif completely. Carefully peel off the stencil. When the paint is dry, align the second stencil over the painted motif and apply the second color through it, referring to your test. If appropriate, repeat to add a third color.

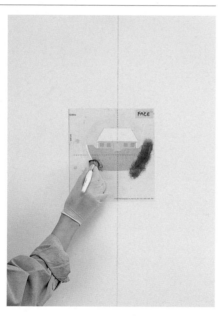

### TIPS FROM THE PROS

• We stippled these small motifs (used a pouncing rather than swirling motion to apply the paint), which explains their lightly dappled appearance. You can stipple through any stencil, although you might find it is more tiring than swirling on the paint if you are doing a large project. Stippling works well if your paint is thin and therefore runny.

• If you are stenciling only one repeat of a complex design, use an artist's palette so that you can put out several colors at once.

**4** Continue, adding the bottom layer of other motifs to your design. Work alternately in different areas to give the paint a chance to dry before you put another stencil on top of it.

**5** When the bottom layer is dry, begin to add the supplementary motifs.

**6** Continue, adding supplementary motifs to other areas.

**7** If you wish, use an artist's brush to add freehand details to your design.

**TIPS FROM THE PROS**
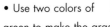
• To add delicate blades of grass, stroke the brush from the base of the blade to the tip. Surprisingly, an old brush with frayed bristles is the perfect tool.
• Use two colors of green to make the grass more interesting.

**8** To add soft details such as clouds, dampen the cosmetic sponge and wring it out. Then dip it into the desired color paint, blot it on a folded paper towel, and press it onto the surface where desired.

**9** Sponged details such as the wispy clouds and rolling sandy hillocks provide a charming frame for this design—and a gentle transition from the scene to a larger, unadorned background.

*A very simple X of leaves, stenciled in two shades of green, forms an allover trellis on this kitchen floor. The lightweight crisscross pattern is a good choice for this narrow space.*

# MURALS AND TROMPE L'OEIL

The terms *mural* and *trompe l'oeil* are often confused. A mural is a design or image painted directly onto a wall; trompe l'oeil is a painting style so realistic that it "tricks the eye," making the viewer believe the object or scene depicted is real. Trompe l'oeil is often painted on walls, but not all murals utilize trompe l'oeil; murals are not necessarily even representational, though we usually think of them as such.

Murals can range in style from realistic and painterly to whimsical or primitive and can incorporate various decorative painting techniques. For instance, a wall can first be colorwashed or ragged, and then a scene can be composed on this background with a combination of stenciled, sponged, stamped, and hand-painted details. Or the wall can be approached as an Old Master's canvas, and each detail created with an artist's brush. Murals often feature landscapes or scenes from history, but they need not be complicated—isolated images, decorative borders, or geometric motifs or patterns can be effective.

Trompe l'oeil is often used to create architectural details that don't exist, such as moldings, medallions, and paneling. The Limestone Blocks technique on pages 132–133 incorporates very simple trompe l'oeil. More elaborate uses include illusionary domed ceilings, book-filled shelves, and windows with curtains blowing into formal gardens. Trompe l'oeil images can be very simple—a vase of flowers painted on the wall above a real shelf, or a framed sign painted on a real door. False cabinets with doors that open to reveal pantry items, frames around real prints that have been glued to the wall, and even a cat watching a mouse hole are traditional trompe l'oeil subjects that can lend charm, elegance, or whimsy to a decor.

Decorative painters who create murals and trompe l'oeil usually have years of art school study and are trained not only in painting techniques but also in preparing and scaling a design. While novices may have luck with stylized murals, more realistic work is difficult to learn from a book. However, an understanding of some of the principles involved will heighten your appreciation for these techniques and perhaps encourage you to try your hand at a simple project or prompt you to enroll in a class.

*Opposite: This sponged stone wall features a trompe l'oeil window opening onto a pastoral landscape, bringing a breath of fresh air and rustic charm to this contemporary kitchen. The potted flowers painted on the windowsill enhance the illusion of depth.*

*Above: The whimsical jungle mural surrounding this window seat forms the perfect backdrop for a young adventurer to sit and daydream. Though the painted area is small, the mural seems expansive because the trees and animals peek from behind the window.*

Landscapes and similar scenes rely upon perspective drawing to convey a sense of depth to the viewer. This is true for many stylized murals as well as realistic ones. When a scene is drawn in perspective, objects that are closer to the viewer are larger, those farther away are smaller, and receding lines that would be parallel in reality converge at the horizon. Here are some things the artist must consider when making a perspective drawing.

**Size** Objects seem to become progressively smaller as they recede into the distance. The painter reduces the scale of objects to indicate their distance from the foreground.

**Color** Objects that are closer to us tend to be more "pure" in color. The same objects appear progressively grayer as they recede into the distance. To paint this transition, you need to add a color's complement and white to the original hue. For instance, if you paint mountains green in the foreground, for each row of mountains behind the first, you should add a little more red and white to the green. Hills, mountains, and similar objects in the very far distance are seen through the earth's atmosphere and appear very blue or lavender; change the paint hues to these colors near the horizon.

**Contrast** The element of contrast in light and shade is very important in depicting distance. The degree of contrast between objects diminishes as they recede from the foreground.

**Texture** Objects that are close to us appear crisp, with sharp details and clearly defined textures. We can't see the details or textures of objects that are far away.

The illusion of depth created with effective use of size, color, contrast, and texture is known as aerial perspective.

## THE VANISHING POINT

The point at which lines converge at the horizon is called the vanishing point, and it enables the artist to judge the relative size of objects as they recede in the picture. Here is a simplified explanation of how to establish the vanishing point for a simple, one-point perspective.

**1** Determine the area the mural will cover. Outline the area on the wall. The bottom edge is often a chair rail or baseboard.

**2** Measure and mark the midpoint of the mural on the bottom edge. This mark represents your point of view for this simple perspective.

**3** Establish the horizon line, which is even with your eye level. Draw a level line across the width of the surface at this point.

**4** Mark the midpoint of the horizon line. This is the vanishing point. Draw a line connecting the midpoint of the bottom edge to the vanishing point. This is the line of sight from your point of view.

**5** Starting at the lower right corner, draw a diagonal line to the vanishing point. Do the same from the lower left corner. Repeat with the upper left and right corners.

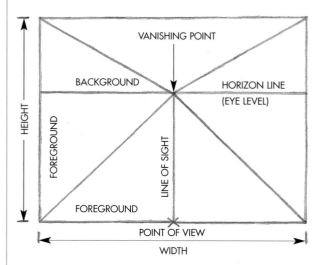

**6** With this framework you can quickly visualize the perspective by imagining how objects would recede toward the vanishing point from all four corners and toward the horizon from the top and bottom edges. The foreground, where objects would be largest, is the area along all four edges of the painting; the background, where objects would be smallest, is the area along the horizon. Once you compose the foreground of your painting, you can project lines from the vanishing point to any objects that have lines from front to back. As these objects reduce in size and converge on the vanishing point, the illusion of depth is achieved.

In the garden scene illustrated at right, you can see the projected lines establishing the front-to-back paths, hedges, and rows of plants. Note, however, that the upright gate and fence pickets remain perpendicular to the bottom edge. The crosswise paths and other side-to-side lines on the receding plane are made successively shorter within the confines of the front-to-back lines, enhancing the feeling of distance. The trees on each side in the foreground are independent objects; their larger size further enhances the illusion of depth. When light and shadow are added to a perspective drawing, this illusion becomes even stronger.

*A trompe l'oeil greenhouse, door ajar, appears to greatly expand the size of this small potting shed. The door on the far end of the greenhouse completes the illusion; you can imagine stepping through the near door into a light-filled space, walking down the plant-filled aisle, and passing out the other door into the misty woods. Note also the painted floor of the potting shed—terrazzo, tile, and rug.*

## TRANSFERRING A DESIGN TO A WALL

Should you wish to try your hand at a mural, first prepare a scale drawing of the design; be sure to measure the surface accurately and include doorways, windows, cabinets, etc. You might be able to make a full-size pattern—for a medallion, small swag, or faux urn, for instance. If not, or if your design calls for a complex arrangement of full-size motifs, work out the design on graph paper. Once you get the basic composition drawn to scale, you might find it helpful to refine it on a larger grid that you draft yourself—or use a computer program. Here are several ways you can transfer the design to your wall.

### TRANSFER PAPER

To transfer a full-size drawing directly to the surface, place a sheet of artist's transfer paper, carbon side down, between the drawing and the surface, and trace over the design with a ballpoint pen or 5H pencil. Because the graphite on the back of the transfer paper will come off with water-base paints, you may want to retrace the lines directly on the wall with a pencil.

### TEMPLATE

If you are working with a simple motif, you can prepare a template and simply trace the outlines onto the wall with a 5H pencil. Use temporary spray adhesive to affix the template while you trace it.

### SCALING UP

If you've made a scale drawing, snap a grid on your wall to correspond to the grid on the drawing (see Stripes and Grids, pages 84–85). Using a 5H pencil, draw the design onto the chalk grid, placing the components of each square on the drawing in the corresponding square on the wall.

### PROJECTING

You can also transfer a design by using a slide projector. Take a slide photograph of your design. Project it onto the wall, adjusting the position of the slide projector until the design fills the space. Then trace around the shapes with a 5H pencil.

## MODELING

Painters use color to "model" objects—to make drawn objects appear three-dimensional. The following terms are used to identify different areas of a modeled object.

**Source of light**  The point or direction from which light is shining on the object. In decorative painting the convention is for the light source to be on the left.

**Form shadow**  The area of the object that is opposite the source of light and therefore darkened.

**Cast shadow**  The shadow that the object casts onto an adjacent surface, opposite the source of light.

**Highlight**  The area of the object that is closest to the source of light and therefore lightened.

**Halftone**  A transparent portion of a highlight or shadow, making a transition between the darkest and lightest areas.

**Accent**  The strongest, most opaque portions of the modeling, representing the brightest or darkest areas of an object. The accent on a shadow has the darkest value; on a highlight it has the lightest value.

**Reflected light**  The light that is reflected back onto the object from the adjacent surface.

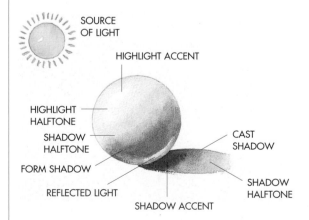

## SHADOW AND ACCENT COLORS

Convincing shadows and highlights are created with varying values of an object's base color. For shadows, add a small amount of lamp black, raw umber, raw sienna, burnt sienna, burnt umber, or Cassel earth to the base color. For highlights, add zinc white.

## TIPS FROM THE PROS

• A good way to tell if the mixture will make a convincing shadow is to dab some on a small brush and hold it so that it casts a shadow on the surface. The color on the brush should closely approximate the color of the shadow.

*Clowns cavort above children's beds in this amusing free-form mural. The green, blue, and white border simulates the awning of a big tent, providing context without depicting an environment. The plain white walls make a perfect backdrop for the explosion of color.*

*A plain, boxy room is transformed by this "primitive" landscape mural. The subdued and monochromatic colors of the pastoral setting promise a peaceful repose. This mural looks impressive, yet the simple perspective, stylized trees, and sponged leaves make it fairly simple to paint.*

Vinegar painting is very like finger painting, with lively patterns worked into a background of wet color—in this case an acrylic glaze made with vinegar. You can manipulate the glaze with almost any small tool you can imagine: a piece of crumpled plastic wrap, an eraser, a comb, a cork, a feather, your finger or fingernail. The technique is by nature imprecise, so exuberant patterns are the norm. When dry, vinegar glaze colors are subdued and matte, but when you varnish them, they return to the vividness they had when wet—so don't be alarmed when you see the colors begin to dull. Here Vinegar Painting is demonstrated on a raised panel door; you can easily adapt the process to different surfaces or create different designs.

## TOOLS

Paint tray with tray liner, roller or brush for base coat
Latex gloves
Small mixing containers
Mixing brush
1" flat nylon artist's brush
1/2" round nylon artist's brush
2"–3" foam brush
3" chip brush
Tools for manipulating glaze (we used fingers and a latex glove)
Paper towels or rags for cleanup

## BASE COAT

Latex flat paint

## GLAZE

1 part artist's acrylic paint (tube, not liquid)
1 part apple cider vinegar
Small amount of acrylic gel retarder (no more than 10% of total mixture)

*We used old rose for the base; vivid red for the principal glaze; and soft black for the accent glaze.*

## SEALER

Oil- or water-base varnish

*Before you begin, read Basics, pages 7–39. Read the following directions all the way through and decide how to adapt them for your surface.*

## TIPS FOR VINEGAR PAINTING

• 1/2 cup glaze is sufficient to paint a door.

• For mysterious reasons, some acrylic colors just don't dissolve in vinegar. If this happens, try another brand or other colors.

• Before you begin glazing your surface, experiment with different colors, tools, and patterns on a piece of prepared tag board (refer to Basics, page 19). If you have a particular pattern in mind, work it out in a space marked to the size of the area to be decorated.

• Vinegar glazes dry relatively quickly. For this reason the technique works best on such items as doors, paneling, floorboards, or boxes or trunks, which have smaller and well-defined surfaces or sections.

• For a more antique look, use a tinted varnish. You can mix varnishes to get a color you like.

• For a floor, apply two or three coats of varnish.

*Right: Country charm abounds on this vinegar-painted door, with fancifully patterned panels set in a stylized wood grain framework. Below: For this shelf, a butter yellow base coat was covered with turquoise and combed. Bottom: Each of these boxes features a dark glaze over a bright base. The green box was decorated with a cut feather (page 137), the brown box with a rubber comb, the blue box in the back with a puff of plastic wrap, and the blue box in the front with a feather quill.*

# VINEGAR PAINTING

**1** Apply the base coat and let it dry for 2 days.

**2** To mix each color glaze, put the acrylic paint into a small container and slowly stir in the vinegar. Add a little retarder. The glaze should have the consistency of buttermilk. If it's too thick, add more vinegar.

**3** With the 1" flat artist's brush, apply the principal (red) glaze to the first area to be decorated, in this instance the raised portion of a door panel.

**TIPS FROM THE PROS**

• If you're doing a floor, apply the glaze to an entire floorboard. Whatever you're decorating, always use its edges to establish the area to cover.

**4** Using the ¹/₂" flat nylon artist's brush, add dots of the accent (black) glaze. To create the pattern shown, place a black dot at each corner and in the center of the panel, an arc of dots inside each corner, and a circle of dots around the center dot. Then pull one finger of a latex glove taut between the thumb and forefinger of each hand (gather the remainder of the glove in the palm of one hand to keep it out of the way). To form a fan design, hold one end of the glove finger on a corner of the panel and, making quick successive movements, tap the glove finger across the glaze in an arc. Repeat at each corner.

**TIPS FROM THE PROS**

• If the glaze is drying too quickly, mix in a little more retarder. You can also brush more vinegar over a section and then rework it.

• If you make a mistake or want to change your design, use the foam brush to wipe out the design and go over it again with your tool. To remove the glaze completely, wipe it off with a paper towel dipped in vinegar.

**5** In the same manner, make a fan design around the center dot; be sure one end of the glove finger is on the center dot when you tap, but adjust your hands as needed to complete the arc.

**6** Outline each fan with closely spaced thumbprint dots, then fill in the remaining space with additional arcs of thumbprints.

**PATTERN IDEAS**

• Consider combing or dragging stripes or swirls into the glaze. For some ideas, see Combing, pages 86–91, or Malachite, pages 158–162.

• Vinegar painting is traditionally used to create highly stylized simulated wood graining. See Mahogany, pages 144–147, Knotty Pine, pages 148–151, and Novelty Tools, pages 136–137, for inspiration and then exaggerate the vein patterns.

**7** Make light strokes with the ¹/₂" artist's brush to "pull out" the accent glaze so that it feathers into the fan patterns.

**8** If the background glaze is not dry to the touch, wait a few minutes until it is before proceeding.

### TIPS FROM THE PROS

• If you'll be adding more glaze to the adjacent areas next, as we did, and you'd prefer to mask the completed area before doing so, be sure to let the glaze dry thoroughly before applying any tape.

• Once a painted section is dry, you can seal it with shellac; this will allow you to wipe off stray brushstrokes.

• If you are painting a door with several panels or a set of cabinet doors, you can repeat the vinegar painting on each remaining panel at this time.

**9** Apply the principal (red) glaze to the next area, in this case, to the recessed portion of the panel. Add a few widely spaced dots of the accent (black) glaze. Create a squiggly line by running your thumbnail through the glaze in a loose zigzag. Let the glaze dry.

**10** Paint a square of the accent glaze in each corner of the recessed panel and also paint the surrounding molding; use whichever brushes work for the size of the area you're painting.

**11** If you are painting a door and you have not completed all panels through step 10, do so. Let the glaze dry.

**12** Working first on the rails and then on the stiles, apply glaze to one section at a time and create a pattern in it. Let the glaze dry before working the adjacent section. We applied the red glaze and used the glove finger to tap on a simple linear pattern reminiscent of wood grain. After your piece has dried thoroughly, apply a coat of varnish.

epending upon the degree to which you take it, Distressing can make a surface look mildy worn or truly beaten up. The more layers of paint you use, the more aged and interesting the effect will appear. You can begin with a new surface, as we did, or work on one that has been previously painted. Various woods react differently to this aging process, so if you can, experiment with the components and steps before committing to a particular working order. You might want to use more or fewer colors, omit the first coat of shellac, sand with different grades of paper—or forgo the fly specks. You can distress furniture and cabinetry by this method too.

*Right: This paneled wall was distressed with multiple layers of brown and blue paint, each sanded away before the next was added. Spots of cream paint were added selectively and sanded.*
*Below: A distressed green glaze covers walls, windows, and desk in this cozy nook.*
*Bottom: Paint that was carefully—and quickly—worn away from these cabinets gives an illusion of age to this farmhouse kitchen.*

## TOOLS

Sandpaper: 60, 180, 220, and 400 grit

Tack cloth

Latex gloves

Two 2"–3" foam brushes

Paint bucket or paint tray and tray liner for base coat

Mixing containers

Stir sticks

3" chip brush or house painter's brush

1" chip brush or flat artist's brush

Spatter stick

Paper towels or rags for cleanup

## SEALER AND FINISH

1 part 3-lb cut shellac, amber or clear

1 part denatured alcohol

## BASE COAT

Latex flat or eggshell paint

## GLAZE

1 part latex flat or eggshell paint

1 part water

*We used* light blue for the base coat; ultramarine blue for the glaze; and dark blue for the spattered accents (we added more ultramarine to the glaze for spattering).

*Before you begin, read Basics, pages 7–39. Also read Spattering, pages 72–75.*

## TIPS FOR DISTRESSING

• The glaze can be thinner and applied in several layers.

• If you want to spatter in a darker value of your glaze, as we did, just add a little more paint to the glaze to deepen the color.

# DISTRESSING

**1** Using the 400-grit sandpaper, lightly sand the surface just to remove any splinters. Wipe with the tack cloth.

**2** If you wish, seal the wood with the shellac and alcohol mixture before painting. Apply the mixture with a foam brush. Let it dry. Lightly sand the surface and wipe with the tack cloth.

**3** Apply the base coat with a chip or house painter's brush. Don't worry if the coverage is not even. Let the paint dry for 1–2 days, as necessary.

**4** Sand the entire surface lightly and irregularly using 220- or 180-grit sandpaper.

**5** Continue sanding, removing more paint in some areas.

**TIPS FROM THE PROS**
• Experiment with different grades of sandpaper to see which you like best, or use several grades to accent the effect.

**6** Mix the first color glaze. With the 3" chip brush, streak the glaze unevenly over the surface. Brush loosely in the direction of the wood grain; if your surface has multiple components, such as rails and stiles, be sure to rotate the brush appropriately.

**7** At this point the distressing is soft rather than rugged. You can stop at this stage if you are pleased with the balance of colors and exposed wood.

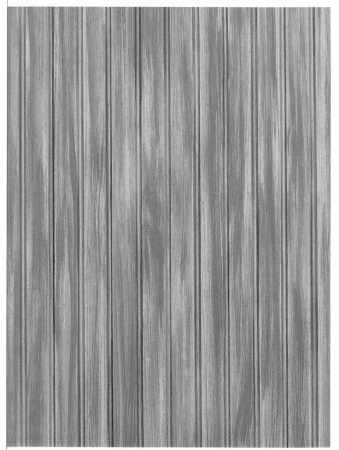

**8** If you wish to further distress the surface, lightly sand it using the 60-grit sandpaper. Sand away more color from selected areas, and feather the edges of the different layers. Wipe the surface with the tack cloth.

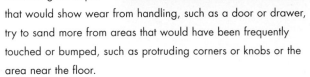

### TIPS FROM THE PROS

• If you are distressing an object that would show wear from handling, such as a door or drawer, try to sand more from areas that would have been frequently touched or bumped, such as protruding corners or knobs or the area near the floor.

**9** With a clean foam brush, apply another coat of the shellac mixture and let it dry.

**10** Lightly sand the surface with the 220-grit sandpaper to dull the sheen. Don't sand through to the previous layers. Wipe the surface with the tack cloth.

**11** If you want to accent the surface with simulated fly specks, mix the accent glaze in a small container and spatter it on with the 1" chip brush or artist's brush; try to create random patterns rather than an allover haze.

**12** The final effect looks worn but not really dirty. Other colors of paint might look older, grubbier, or just different.

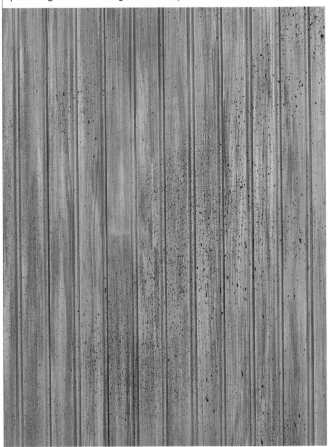

**P**ickling is the process of lightly staining unfinished wood with a colored glaze; it simulates the traditional technique of liming. Pickling is often used for floors and paneling in informal decors, and creates an airy, summery ambience. Though white is a typical color, any pastel would be effective, and commercial pickling stains are available in many hues, should you not want to mix your own glaze. You can also pickle unfinished furniture, doors, or cabinets; be sure to seal the surface afterward in a manner appropriate to its use.

*Right: Pickled beaded wainscoting set against pink walls is fresh and summery—great for a real or would-be cottage. Below: A hardwood strip floor is disguised by a large checkerboard pickled in pastel colors. The floor adds a light and playful balance to the dark cabinets and oak furniture.*

### TOOLS

Sandpaper: 220 and
   400 grit
Latex gloves
Tack cloth
Mixing container
Stir sticks
Paint tray and tray liner
3" foam brush
Paper towel roll(s)
Paper towels or rags for
   cleanup

### GLAZE

2 parts latex paint
3 parts water

*Or commercially prepared pickling stain*

### FINISH

Polyurethane or varnish,
   as desired

*We used off-white for the glaze.*

*Before you begin, read Basics, pages 7–39.*

### TIPS FOR PICKLING

• Always apply the glaze to your surface in a logical manner, working on one component at a time and stopping at natural seams.
• If you are pickling a large, unbroken surface, you may find it easier to achieve seamless coverage with an oil-base glaze.

# PICKLING

**1** Sand the surface to remove any splinters and roughness. Wipe with a tack cloth.

**2** Mix the glaze. Pour some into the paint tray. Apply the glaze with the foam brush, brushing in the direction of the wood grain. If your surface has multiple components, such as rails and stiles, be sure to rotate the brush appropriately.

**3** Immediately wipe off the glaze. Use a folded or wadded paper towel and wipe in the direction of the wood grain.

**TIPS FROM THE PROS**
• If you are pickling a grooved surface like the bead board shown here, you'll probably find it easier to pickle each flat area and then immediately touch up the preceding bead; use the side of the brush and then wipe off the glaze. Don't wait to touch up all the beads at the end; do each while the surrounding glaze is still wet.

**4** At this point the natural wood grain pattern should show quite clearly through the light stain. Of course, the effect will vary with the type of wood and glaze color. You can stop at this stage if you are pleased with the balance of color and wood grain.

**5** If you'd prefer an effect with more color and less wood grain, apply a second coat of the glaze and wipe it off as before.

**6** With a second coat of glaze, the color is more opaque, and less of the natural wood grain shows. If you were to apply a third coat, you'd probably obscure the grain completely—you'd just have painted woodwork.

*Pickling adds a delicate but interesting finish to woodwork, appropriate to both new and old interiors. These shutters have been pickled and lightly distressed, a treatment that sits comfortably with the pale colorwashed walls and rustic rough-hewn beams.*

# CRACKLING

**P**aint that has been exposed to weather or left for long periods in an abandoned house often cracks in an interesting random pattern. You can replicate this effect with a commercial weathered crackling product, which, when applied between coats of paint, will cause the top paint to crack and reveal the base coat. The more contrast between your base coat and top coat, the more dramatic the crackle effect will be. Because it's impossible to predict exactly how the paint will crack or to control the pattern, you must be willing to enjoy whatever effect results from the process. Different products require specific paints, so refer to our directions as a general guide, but use the paint indicated on the label.

*Right: Used judiciously, weathered crackle can add interest to woodwork or furnishings without making them appear worn out. The raw wood of this new built-in cabinet was given an upbeat green crackle finish. Below: A brand-new door with a crackle finish looks rugged and weathered, perfectly suiting this western home. The crackled white paint was aged with a dark brown wash.*

## TOOLS
Paint bucket, rack, brushes, and roller for base coat
Latex gloves
Mixing containers
Stir sticks
2" foam or nylon house painter's brushes
Paper towels or rags for cleanup

## BASE AND TOP COATS
Latex flat or eggshell paint

## CRACKLING MEDIUM

## FINISH
Polyurethane or product recommended by the crackling medium manufacturer

*We used chestnut for the base coat; cream for the top coat.*

*Before you begin, read Basics, pages 7–39.*

## TIPS FOR CRACKLING
• Crackling is difficult to control, and the precise effect is unpredictable. You might be happiest using this technique on small items or on surfaces with multiple components, such as panel doors, chests of drawers, or paneling, where you can brush between the seams. Use common sense to choose brush sizes that match the component's width.

• If you wish to crackle a whole wall, consider crackling it in segments. Refer to Stripes and Grids, pages 84–85, and following steps 2 and 3 of the directions, crackle alternate segments first, then repeat for the remaining segments.

• Be sure your surface is primed before applying the base coat.

# CRACKLING

**1** Apply the base coat and let it dry for 2 days.

**2** With a foam brush, apply an even coat of crackling medium. Let it dry as directed on the product label. The medium is clear, so it doesn't change the base-coat color. If you look closely, you'll see cracks in the dry surface.

**3** Apply the top coat of paint with a clean foam brush, brushing in one direction only. The paint will crackle as you apply it. Work from top to bottom in the longest possible strokes; try not to overlap previously brushed areas when adding consecutive sections. Brush in the direction of the wood grain. If your surface has multiple components, such as rails and stiles, be sure to rotate the brush.

**TIPS FROM THE PROS**

• When the wet paint overlaps, it lifts from the surface and creates smears like the one next to the painter's hand in the photo. The only way to correct this is to wash off the paint and crackling medium with water and start again.

• A few smears might not bother you, but too many will make the effect look phony rather than faux.

• If you apply the top coat with a roller instead of a brush, the crackling will be finer than it is when the paint is brushed on. Be careful not to reroll the paint as you apply it.

**4** The completed surface is covered with irregularly cracked paint. At this point you should seal the surface with the recommended product or continue with one of the following variations.

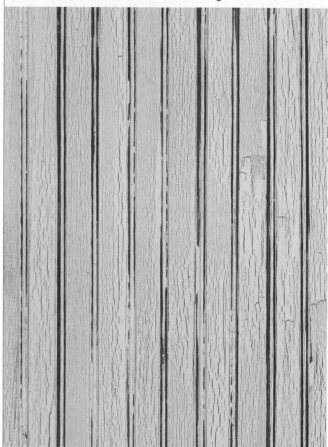

**PORCELAIN CRACKLING**

• Another type of crackling, traditionally called *cracquelure*, features very fine cracks, or crazing, like those seen on some porcelain or tile surfaces. You can purchase commercial products that produce this effect also. Porcelain crackling is as unpredictable as weathered crackling. Because it is delicate, it is nearly imperceptible from a distance, but it can be very attractive on small items.

• For a more antique look, apply two coats of amber shellac after the top coat has dried. Let the shellac dry between coats.

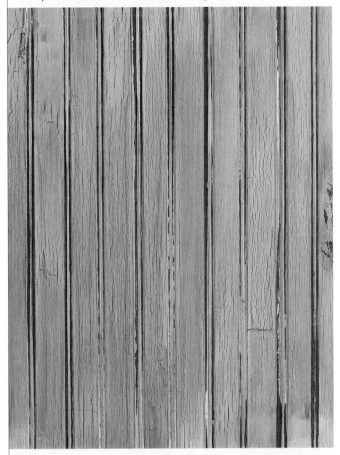

*Flat walls are not easy to crackle, and this checkerboard of alternating horizontal and vertical brush strokes offers a good—but tedious—way to utilize the hard-to-control medium. To replicate this effect, crackle alternate squares and seal them before crackling the remaining portions.*

• Here the crackled paint surface has been dressed up with a wash of phthalo blue artist's oil paint. To do this, first mix 1 part thinner and 1 part linseed oil. Pour 2 tablespoons of this medium into an empty tuna can and add 2 drops of japan drier. Squeeze some of the paint onto an artist's palette. Dip a rag in the medium and then into the color. Rub it onto the crackled surface in one direction, creating streaks of bright blue. If you prefer to wash your surface with latex or acrylic paint instead of artist's oil paint, be sure to seal it first with clear shellac, or the water-base medium will remove the crackling.

There are many kinds and colors of granite; the gray one demonstated here is especially easy to replicate. In fact, it's just a three-color sponging process finished with spattering, but the tiny dots of color covering the surface look like the grains for which granite is named. This granite is an excellent choice for faux tiles because it has no veins to stop or start at grout lines. Plain shaft pillars, simple baseboards, and tabletops would also be enhanced with a granite finish. Stay away from fluted or relief surfaces; they're hard to sponge.

*Right: Faux granite is an excellent choice for reviving flea market finds. Here it transforms an old Arts & Crafts–style plant stand. Below: This inexpensive wooden salad bowl, painted with a rose-colored granite finish, masquerades as an example of upscale contemporary craft— right at home against the faux granite tiled wall. Of course, painted pieces should not be used for serving food.*

## TOOLS

Paint bucket, rack, brushes, and roller for base coat
Chalk line
Latex gloves
Mixing containers
Stir sticks
Paint tray with 3 tray liners
$1/16"$–$1/4"$ masking tape
Large sea sponge(s)
Bucket of water
3" chip brush
Spatter stick
Paper towels or rags for cleanup

## BASE COAT

Latex eggshell or satin paint

## GLAZES

1 part latex satin paint
1 part water

*Or commercially prepared glaze*

*We used* medium gray for the base coat; light gray, dark gray, terra-cotta, and black for the glazes.

## FINISH

Low-luster to semigloss varnish, as desired

*Before you begin, read Basics, pages 7–39. Also read Sponging, pages 66–71, and Spattering, pages 72–75. Be sure to test the technique on tag board, bristol board, or a portion of your surface.*

## TIPS FOR GRANITE

• If you are painting a small area, use artist's acrylics and follow the directions for mixing Acrylic Glaze #1 on page 16.

• Use a sea sponge with a rough pointy surface—it will create smaller, more realistic dots of color.

• The order in which you apply the different color glazes isn't critical but does affect the final painting. You can add more of any or all colors later. Experiment to see which order is most pleasing.

• It's best to apply each color paint to the entire wall at once. However, this is a sponging process, so you can stop and start if you need to. Use common sense about cleaning the sponge whenever you change colors, or use a different sponge for each color.

• Each color should be dry to the touch before you add the next. Latex glaze dries quickly, and you can probably begin subsequent coats promptly as long as you always begin at the same edge.

# GRANITE

**1** Mask the area adjacent to where your granite will go. Apply the base coat and let it dry for 2 days.

**2** If you are making faux tiles, plan their size and layout. The tiles shown are 12" × 12" with $^1/_{16}$" grout lines on a regular grid. Measure the grid and mark it on your surface by snapping the chalk line. Apply narrow tape to the grid, placing it consistently above or below and to the left or right of the marked lines. (See Stripes and Grids, pages 84–85.)

**TIPS FROM THE PROS**

• Granite tiles are usually butted together, so that little or no grout shows. Use the narrowest tape you can find to set up your grid. Or if you have a steady hand, you can omit the tape grid, paint the granite, and then hand-paint a grid of thin lines to create a tile effect.

**3** Mix the dark gray glaze and pour some into a lined paint tray. Dip a sponge in the water, wring it out, and dip it into the glaze. Sponge on the glaze evenly but not densely all over the surface. Let the paint dry.

**TIPS FROM THE PROS**

• If you'll be sponging on more than one color in a work session, keep the sponges you're not using in the bucket of water so that they don't dry out. Wring them out before using.

• If you do this, you won't have to clean the sponges between uses, but do use a separate sponge for each color.

**4** Repeat with the light gray glaze. Let it dry.

**5** Repeat with the terra-cotta glaze. Let it dry.

**6** Stand back before you continue, to see where you would like to create darker or lighter areas. Then sponge on more dark gray glaze where desired. Let this glaze dry.

**7** Repeat where desired with the light gray glaze. Let it dry.

**TIPS FROM THE PROS**
• You can add more terra-cotta at this time if you wish; we chose not to.

**8** Mix the black glaze and spatter it on using the chip brush. Direct your spattering so that you create small clouds of color with a swirled pattern overall.

**9** Spatter on the terra-cotta glaze, creating some areas of more density and some areas of less density. Let the painted surface dry for 24 hours.

**10** Finish with your choice of varnish. Let dry according to the manufacturer's directions. If you have made tiles, remove the tape.

**11** These tiles would be a great choice for floors, as well as walls, in a foyer, bath, or home office.

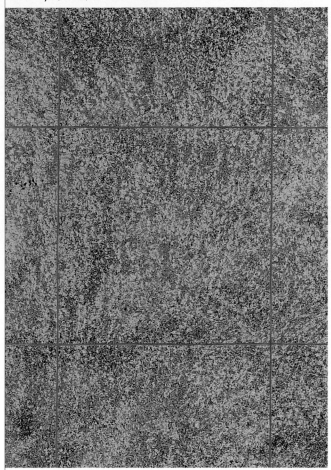

Though trompe l'oeil stone walls look intricate, they're really just sponged and spattered grids finished with simple highlights. The most difficult aspect of a stone wall is setting up the grid—figuring the size and repeat of the blocks, marking them on your surface, and applying masking tape. Of course, there's no requirement that the blocks be identical; an irregular repeat will look rustic; a regular repeat, more sophisticated.

*Right: A painted stone wall provides a monumental setting for opulent furnishings. The amber cast of the stone looks especially attractive with the gilt details. Below: Faux stone blocks add to the stature of this plain column. Resin and plaster columns are readily available at home centers.*

## TOOLS

3" brown paper painter's tape

Paint bucket, rack, brushes, and roller for base coat

Chalk line

Pencil

1/4" masking tape

Latex gloves

Mixing containers

Stir sticks

Paint tray with 3 tray liners

Large sea sponge(s)

Bucket of water

3" chip brush

Veiner or small chip brush

Artist's palette

Touch-up brush

Spatter stick

Lightweight straightedge (optional)

Paper towels or rags for cleanup

## BASE COAT

Latex flat or eggshell paint

## GLAZES

1 part latex flat paint

1 part water

*Or* commercially prepared glaze.

## ARTIST'S ACRYLIC

Raw umber (or any dark brown)

*We used* off-white for the base coat; light beige, medium beige, and dark beige for the glazes.

*Before you begin, read Basics, pages 7–39. Also read Sponging, pages 66–71, and Spattering, pages 72–75.*

### TIPS FOR LIMESTONE

• Stone can have a pink, green, blue, yellow, or gray cast. Find the basic color you'd like on a house paint sample strip. Then select three consecutive values.

• It's best to apply each color paint to the entire wall at once. However, this is a sponging process, so you can stop and start if you need to. Use common sense about cleaning the sponge whenever you change colors, or use a different sponge for each color.

• Latex paints are lighter in color when wet than dry, so it can be difficult to tell where you've applied them when they are close in value, as these are. Avoid confusion by using a different paint tray for each glaze, numbering them #1, #2, and #3.

• Each color should be dry to the touch before you add the next. Latex glaze dries quickly, and you can probably begin subsequent coats promptly as long as you begin each at the same edge.

# LIMESTONE BLOCKS

**1** Mask the areas adjacent to where your stone will go. Apply the base coat and let it dry for 2 days.

**2** Plan your block size and layout. The blocks shown are 12" × 15" with ¹/₄" grout lines on a staggered layout. Mark the horizontal courses for the stone blocks by snapping chalk lines. Then mark the vertical dividing lines with a pencil. Apply narrow tape to the grid, placing the tape consistently either above or below and to the left or right of the marked lines. (See Stripes and Grids, pages 84–85.)

**3** Mix the darkest beige glaze and pour some into a lined paint tray. Dip a sponge in the water, wring it out, and dip it into the glaze. Sponge paint the surface, creating some denser areas, some more open areas, and some areas that are completely open. Let the paint dry.

**4** Repeat with the medium beige, filling in some of the empty areas.

**TIPS FROM THE PROS**

• The colors are close in hue, so if you have trouble keeping track of where you've added the second glaze, stand back and look at your taped grid— the more glaze you add, the less of the tape you'll see.

• If you'll be sponging on more than one color in a work session, keep the sponges you're not using in the bucket of water so that they don't dry out. Wring them out before using.

**5** Repeat with the lightest beige, filling in the open areas so that there are definite lighter and darker areas.

**6** If you think the overall effect needs areas of greater contrast, create them by sponging on more of any color in selected areas.

**TIPS FROM THE PROS**

• To keep the stone blocks distinct, don't let areas of contrast continue across the tape lines. If you apply paint over the tape at this time, turn the sponge over and blot off the unwanted portion.

**7** Take up some of the medium beige glaze on the veiner or small chip brush and drag it laterally across various areas to create wavy veins. Pat immediately with the clean side of the sponge. Make sure each vein starts and stops within or at the edge of a block. (The vein color is exaggerated here for photography.)

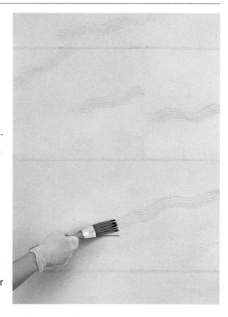

**8** Place the raw umber artist's acrylic on the artist's palette. Dip the veiner or chip brush in water, then mix the paint to watercolor consistency. Drag on more wavy veins and pat with the sponge as before.

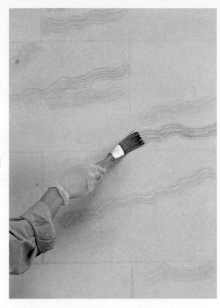

**9** On your palette, mix some raw umber with any one of the beige glazes. Take up some of the paint on the chip brush and spatter across the stone blocks.

**TIPS FROM THE PROS**

• Add more veining at this time if you'd like.

• You can spatter all over or just in some areas. Spatter especially over any areas you think look too spongy or too crisp.

• To add nuance, pounce some of the spatters with the tip of the chip brush; blot other areas with the sponge.

• You can spatter as much as you'd like, and with all three beige glazes. In fact, the more spattering you do, the more realistic the effect will be—as long as the spattering is done in a thoughtful way.

**10** Remove the tape. Let the paint dry completely. Erase any exposed pencil lines.

**11** If you wish, create realistic dimension by adding shadow lines to the bottom and right edges of each block. Use a touch-up brush and raw umber and water mixed to watercolor consistency on your palette. Let it dry.

**TIPS FROM THE PROS**

• To help steady your hand, hold a lightweight straightedge tipped at an angle away from the wall as a guide for keeping your brush steady and the accent line straight.

**12** The completed wall appears softly textured with subtle color variations. Other trompe l'oeil stone effects include wedges, keystones, and quoins (cornerstones)—you can insert these around doors or windows on a wall with block courses or one that has been sponged all over to simulate stucco.

## TRICKS OF THE TRADE
# NOVELTY TOOLS

Cruise the aisles of a paint store, and you'll see quite a variety of special glazing tools. Here are some ideas for using three of them. Of course, the colors you choose will influence the mood of your finish, so consider a palette that feels lighthearted, sophisticated, antique, or for the wood grain, realistic, as you wish.

For each of these techniques, first apply a base coat and let it dry. Use common sense to mask areas adjacent to the surface you're painting. You can use any of the basic glazes (see page 16 for the recipes) or commercially prepared glazes. Mix the glazes and pour them into paint trays fitted with liners as you need them. Before you begin, read Basics, pages 7–39, for general information on applying glaze, safety, and cleanup.

### NOVELTY ROLLER

This three-color finish has an irregular allover pattern reminiscent of a random mosaic; with these colors the effect is watery and would be pretty in a bath or on a porch. The pattern was created with a foam roller with a honeycomb surface (these rollers usually require special handles).

**1** Using the novelty roller, roll on the first glaze in a haphazard pattern; fill the entire ground, rolling in various directions with slightly overlapping paths. Let the paint dry.

**TIPS FROM THE PROS**
• If the paint seems thick or begins to drip in some spots, blot it with a paper towel.

**2** With a clean honeycomb roller, roll on a couple of widths of the second glaze—the goal is to off-load the roller but not completely empty it. Immediately wipe off the glaze with wadded paper towels, leaving a thin wash of color over the first pattern.

**3** With the roller barely loaded with the second glaze, roll on a haphazard pattern as before.

**TIPS FROM THE PROS**
• Develop a rhythm for applying, wiping, and then applying more of the second glaze. If you don't feel comfortable, use a foam hot-dog roller to stipple the surface (see page 58) and then roll on the top honeycomb pattern with a nearly empty roller.
• You'll probably have better luck using several rollers so that you will have various amounts of glaze available at any time.

**4** Continue to roll on, wipe off, and roll again until the entire surface is lightly patterned.

### FEATHER

A whimsical effect can be scratched into wet glaze with a turkey feather, which was the tool used to create the random cone and swirl design shown opposite. If you'd like to duplicate the subtle coloration of the sample, sponge a contrasting glaze over the base coat (see pages 68–69) and let it dry before applying the glaze you will scratch. In addition to a low-nap roller, you'll need a 3" chip brush and several turkey feathers, which are available in paint and craft supply stores.

**1** Using scissors, trim the barbs on the inside curve of each feather so that they extend about $3/8$" from the quill (see the photo on page 10). Snip the point off the end of the quill.

**2** Roll on two roller widths of glaze from the ceiling to the floor. Drag off some of the glaze with the chip brush (see pages 76–79, but don't worry about dragging perfectly straight lines). Be sure to leave a wet edge.

**3** Hold the cut edge of the feather against the surface and move it through the glaze in an arc, making a conical shape. Repeat at random, varying the angle. When the feather becomes loaded with glaze, wipe it on a paper towel.

**4** Using the end of the quill, draw random spirals between the cones. Repeat the process until the entire surface is patterned.

### GRAINING PAD

There are various textured rubber graining pads, rollers, and squeegees that make a simulated wood grain when dragged through wet glaze. To use any one of these, pull it through the glaze, rocking it up and down as you go. The speed at which you pull and the frequency of rocking together make possible infinite but somewhat unpredictable variations of a basic imprint. The patterns made by the different tools vary more in width than in detail, so experiment with one before investing in an assortment. Here we alternated passes of a small squeegee and a graduated rubber comb. You'll also need a low-nap roller and a 3" chip brush.

**1** Roll on two roller widths of glaze from the ceiling to the floor. Drag off some of the glaze with the chip brush (see pages 76–79, but don't worry about dragging perfectly straight lines). Be sure to leave a wet edge.

**2** Starting at the ceiling, hold the rocking tool with the heel against the surface and pull it down in one continuous motion, rocking from the heel toward the head and back several times to produce a heart grain pattern.

### TIPS FROM THE PROS

• Pull the tool down quickly and rock it slowly. It takes some practice to get the motion right.

• You can also drag in a basketweave pattern (see page 90) to create a parquet effect.

**3** Repeat, using a rocking tool or rubber comb, as you wish. When you near the wet edge, roll on two more roller widths of glaze and repeat the process.

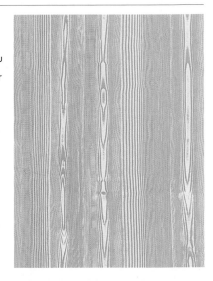

**W**ell-painted wood grain is so convincing that you can stand next to it without realizing it's faux. While graining certainly takes skill, judgment plays an equal role—you have to know what the wood looks like and make subtle adjustments to your work in order to bring out realistic pattern and color. You can gain skill by practicing the following directions; judgment comes with observation of real wood and familiarity with the artist's materials. Wood grain is generally painted on woodwork or items that could be fashioned from wood. If you want to grain a wall, you should break it into sections and create simple trompe l'oeil boards or panels.

We explain three wood grains here. Burl is one of the easiest woods to paint; the technique is a variant of Rubbing and Ragging, with some painterly accents. Real burl is cut from domed growths on a variety of trees; we've chosen walnut, but you can experiment with colors to mimic blonder woods. For Mahogany you work on a coat of wet glaze, wiping off portions to "reveal" the characteristic vein patterns. The process is complex, but because the glaze is wet, you can brush out mistakes and try again—up to a point. For Knotty Pine you paint the veins one by one onto a dry background, so good brush control is essential.

**TOOLS FOR ALL**
Paint tray and brushes for
    base coat
Latex gloves
Stir sticks
Sandpaper: 220–400 grit
Tack cloth
Painter's masking tape
Mixing containers
Artist's palette
Palette knife
Paper towels and rags
Sketch paper and marker
    or carpenter's pencil
Empty, clean tuna can

Additional tools, brushes,
paints, mediums, and
finishes are listed with each
technique.

*Before you begin, read
Basics, pages 7–39 and
Getting Started, page 140.
Practice your chosen
technique first on paper
(see page 19).*

*Immediately submerge
oil- or solvent-soiled rags in
water. Discard according
to local ordinances.*

*Right: This bookcase was
grained with stylized
Mahogany; the plainer
portions were flogged.
Use the colors for Burl
to replicate this effect.
Below: The walls of this
study were dragged to
simulate a simple wood
grain; experiment with
fan, veiner, and chip
brushes to produce this
kind of pattern.
Bottom: Fake pickled
log walls were outlined,
sponged, rubbed, and
lightly grained over a
white base.*

# WOOD GRAINING

## GETTING STARTED

- The graining directions specify that acrylic and oil glazes be used at various times so that you can work efficiently and easily. For best results, use the glaze specified and seal the surface as directed. Read Using the Artist's Palette, page 17.
- If you are graining a surface with multiple sections, such as a paneled door, complete all the steps indicated on a single section before proceeding to another section, as specified in the technique directions. When all sections have been completed, proceed to the next part of the graining, as directed.
- If you are graining a door, read Painting Doors, page 29, to see the order in which to work.
- If you feel confident, you can work on a center stile immediately after working on an adjacent panel, as we did; this will cut down on drying time. If you do not feel confident, mask all sides of each panel before graining it.
- As you work, use common sense about masking adjacent areas and be sure to remove tape whenever you stop to let the paint dry. Touch up any seepage immediately. Be sure the paint is dry before you mask over it.
- Clean up at the end of each day and prepare additional medium and paint as needed.

## BURL

### ADDITIONAL TOOLS
Two 3" chip brushes
Fan brush
1/2" short-bristled artist's brush
2" softener (brush) (optional)

### ARTIST'S OILS
Burnt umber
Raw umber
Burnt sienna
Ivory black

### BASE COAT
Latex or alkyd satin paint,
    warm beige

### FINISH
Low-luster to semigloss varnish,
    as desired

### MEDIUM
1 part linseed oil
1 part thinner
Japan drier (added later)

**1** Apply the base coat and let it dry, 2 days for latex, 2–3 days for alkyd. Lightly sand. Wipe with a tack cloth.

**2** Pour 2 tablespoons of the medium into a tuna can. Dip a piece of paper towel in the medium and wipe it all over the prepared surface. Then add 2 drops of japan drier to the medium in the can.

**3** On your palette, squeeze out, in descending quantity, a small amount of burnt umber, raw umber, burnt sienna, and a bit of black. Dip a chip brush into the medium, then pick up some of each artist's oil in order, mix on the palette, and brush onto the surface in a crisscross fashion. Repeat to cover the surface. There should be some darker and some lighter areas.

**4** Scrunch up a paper towel and dab it all over the glaze, twisting it on the surface to create a swirled pattern. Lightly whisk a clean chip brush over the surface to soften the effect, and let the paint dry.

### TIPS FROM THE PROS
- Using the same colors, we dragged straight grain on the stile to the right of the panel as soon as we completed the burl graining.

**5** Dip the fan brush in the medium. Blot the excess on a piece of paper towel and then pick up burnt umber, raw umber, and black; mix together. Snake the brush around some, but not all, of the swirls to give them greater definition.

**TIPS FROM THE PROS**

• Practice will teach you how much medium to use. The amount depends on what is mixed on your palette and what is on the surface you're graining.

• You should be practically dry-brushing the glaze onto the surface; the glaze should not be at all runny.

**6** Soften the newly painted areas with the second chip brush.

**7** Dip the short-bristled brush into the mixed colors on the palette and then into more paint if needed (but not into the medium) and dab on clusters of small dots to represent tiny knots in the darker areas.

**8** To create highlights, tap each knot lightly with your thumbnail.

**9** Soften with the softener or second chip brush.

**TIPS FROM THE PROS**

• If you'd like, before allowing the surface to dry, you can add a few more swirls with the fan brush, working as before.

• You can also add more knots at this time.

**10** Remove any tape. Clean all equipment. Let the graining dry overnight. If there are other areas of your item to be grained, take each to this stage before proceeding.

**11** Pour 2 tablespoons of medium into a clean tuna can and add 2 drops of japan drier. On your palette, squeeze out, in descending quantity, a small amount of burnt umber, raw umber, burnt sienna, and a tiny bit of black. Dip a clean chip brush into the medium, then pick up some of each artist's oil in order, mix on the palette, and brush onto the surface in a crisscross fashion. Repeat to cover the surface.

**TIPS FROM THE PROS**

• The glaze should be transparent, adding just a haze of color.

**12** Scrunch up a paper towel and dab and twist it over the surface as before. To refine the pattern, take more glaze off some areas than others. If you'd like an area to become darker, pounce on a little more glaze with the loaded brush used in the previous step and then towel it. Soften with the chip brush as you go.

**TIPS FROM THE PROS**
• Don't pick up more glaze from your palette at this point, or you'll risk "opening" the pattern.

**13** Hold the chip brush at a 45° angle to the surface. Using a series of short, interrupted strokes, pull the brush down through the glaze in areas where there are no knots, creating a ladder pattern of undulations.

**14** If you feel there are flat areas that lack definition, use the fan brush and the glaze already mixed on your palette to snake more lines into them. You can also create more knots by dipping the short-bristled brush into the artist's oils and then tapping it around the existing knots, as well as on some other darker areas.

**TIPS FROM THE PROS**
• If the graining starts to "open up," soften immediately with a chip brush—you can use a clean brush or the one loaded with paint, depending on the area that's opening.
• You can also gently pounce out glaze that is opening; use the tip of a chip brush.

**15** If there are other areas of your item to be grained, take each to this stage before proceeding. Let each dry.

**16** Varnish the grained surface to intensify the color and protect the painting.

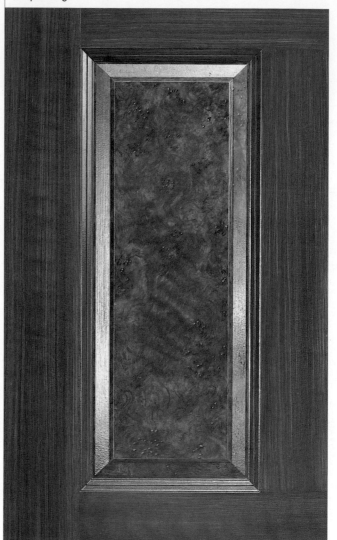

# TRICKS OF THE TRADE
## FLOGGING

Flogging is an easy technique that creates a small-scale allover pattern. Although flogging is customarily used only to create pores for wood graining, there is no reason you can't use it alone on a wall, where it will appear textured, like bark or shagreen (sharkskin). To flog, you repeatedly slap the flat side of a special long-bristled brush, called a flogger, onto wet glaze. You work from the bottom to the top of the area you're painting, covering only one brush width in each pass, so flogging a large area may tire your wrist.

### TOOLS

Paint bucket, rack, brushes, and roller for base coat

3" brown paper painter's tape

Latex gloves

Mixing bucket

Paint tray with tray liner

Stir sticks

9" low-nap roller with handle

Curved painter's tool

2" foam brush

3" (or wider) flogger

Paper towels or rags for cleanup

### BASE COAT

Latex or alkyd satin paint

### GLAZE

1 part alkyd glazing liquid

1 part paint thinner or mineral spirits

1 part alkyd paint

Small amount of linseed oil

*Or commercially prepared glaze or Latex or Acrylic Glaze, page 16*

*We used very pale gray for the base coat; medium gray for the glaze.*

*Before you begin, read Basics, pages 7–39.*

*Immediately submerge oil- or solvent-soiled rags in water. Discard according to local ordinances.*

**1** Apply the base coat and let it dry, 2 days for latex, 2–3 days for alkyd.

**2** Mask the walls, ceiling, and baseboards adjacent to where you'll be working. Mix the glaze; it should have the consistency of heavy cream. Pour some of the glaze into the paint tray.

### TIPS FROM THE PROS

• Practice first on a sheet of paper taped to the wall to determine the most comfortable distance for you to stand.

**3** Cut in the first corner (refer to Basics, page 23); start at the ceiling and use the foam brush to apply the glaze. Also cut in for 18" along the ceiling and baseboard. Roll two roller widths of glaze from top to bottom, reloading as needed.

**4** Hold the flogger parallel to the wall with the bristles straight up. Starting at the bottom corner, slap the bristles onto the wall, moving continuously up the wall in quick successive motions. Put the most pressure at the ferrule. The impressions should overlap slightly.

**5** Clean your brush on a rag when it becomes loaded with paint. Once you reach the top, return to the bottom and repeat; the splayed bristles should slightly overlap the previous pass. Continue, flogging the rest of the applied glaze; do not flog the leading edge.

**6** Cut in another 18" section along the ceiling and baseboard adjacent to the first section. Roll two roller widths of glaze from top to bottom, reloading as needed. Starting at the bottom edge of the area you just completed, flog the adjacent section.

**7** Notice the evenness of the pattern. You should not see any space between the brush impressions.

# MAHOGANY

## ADDITIONAL TOOLS

House painter's brush(es)
3" flogger
3" foam brush
3" chip brush(es)
Burlap scrap (or coarse paper towel)
Lint-free cloth scrap (or soft paper towel)
1/2" short-bristled artist's brush
2"–3" softener (brush) (optional)
2" fan brush or veiner

## BASE COAT

Alkyd satin paint, peachy orange

## FLOGGING GLAZE

1 part raw umber artist's acrylic
1 part Payne's gray artist's acrylic
2 parts acrylic medium
1–2 parts water

## MEDIUM #1

1 part linseed oil
2 parts thinner
Japan drier (added later)

## MEDIUM #2

1 part oil
1 part thinner
Japan drier (added later)

## ARTIST'S OILS

Burnt sienna
Burnt umber
Alizarin crimson

## FINISHES

3-lb cut clear shellac
Denatured alcohol
Low-luster to semigloss varnish, as desired

---

**1** Apply the base coat and let it dry, 2 days for latex, 2–3 days for alkyd. Lightly sand. Wipe with a tack cloth.

---

**2** Read Flogging, page 143. Mask the area adjacent to where you'll begin. Mix the flogging glaze and apply it using a house painter's brush. Then, using the flogger, flog the exposed surface. Repeat as needed until the surface is covered with small "pores." Let it dry.

**3** While you are waiting, sketch a graining pattern on a piece of paper of roughly the same proportions as the area to be grained.

### TIPS FROM THE PROS

• You'll need a different pattern for each principal section. Narrow sections such as rails and stiles can have simple straight graining, for which no pattern is necessary.

---

**4** If appropriate, repeat step 2 on each remaining section of the surface.

### TIPS FROM THE PROS

• If you are painting a door or similar object, flog in the direction of the grain—turn the brush 90° and flog crosswise on horizontal components.

---

**5** To seal the flogged surface, mix equal parts of denatured alcohol and 3-lb cut shellac; apply the mixture with the foam brush. Let it dry.

---

**6** Squeeze a small amount of each artist's oil onto the palette. Pour 6 tablespoons of medium #1 into the tuna can and add 4 drops of japan drier. Dip the chip brush into the medium and then pick up a little of each color. Brush the glaze onto the surface with crisscross strokes, then drag the brush over the surface in the direction of the grain.

### TIPS FROM THE PROS

• Pick up more red or brown oil color, as you like.
• You can brush the glaze loosely over the whole section and then drag it out.

**7** Scrunch up the burlap scrap and pinch it between your fingers. Starting at the bottom, roughly draw in the peaks only of the heart-grain portion of your pattern. Round the apexes slightly. The lines will be very sketchy.

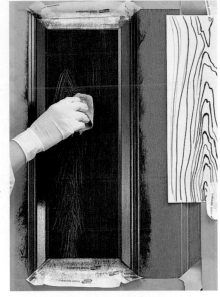

### TIPS FROM THE PROS

• Give the peaks some movement. Avoid making them perfectly regular, symmetrical, or aligned.

• Even professionals would find it difficult to add veins to the recesses of a panel like this—there is too much else to do while the glaze is wet. Just leave the dragged glaze in any small recesses as is.

**8** With the burlap, extend the sides of each peak toward the bottom. Work from the lowest peak up. Be careful not to let the pattern grow progressively wider as it works downward.

**9** Drag the burlap from top to bottom alongside the heart grain to form the side grain. Repeat, gradually straightening the lines as they become farther from the heart grain.

**10** Wrap the lint-free cloth or paper towel around your thumb and trace over some of the sketched peaks to refine them. Move your thumb up and down in a sketchy manner to add depth as well as width to these highlights.

**11** Crush the cloth or paper towel between your fingers and gently wipe off a little of the glaze from some areas of the side grain. Always start at the top and wipe all the way to the end of the sketched vein; allow the cloth to trail off rather than lifting it partway down.

**12** Dip the short-bristled brush into the medium and then pick up some of each artist's oil; paint in some darker accents above the peak highlights. Whisk the brush in short up and down movements to add depth as well as width to these accents.

**13** Soften the heart grain by lightly stroking with the previously used chip brush from the open end toward the peak. If your design has peaks pointing up and down, as in the photo, stroke from the bottom up to the dividing area and then from the top down. Then, following the vein direction, soften the side grain.

**TIPS FROM THE PROS**

• Soften any panel recesses at this time as well; use a smaller brush.

**14** Dip the short-bristled brush into the medium and then pick up some of each artist's oil, mixing in more of the burnt umber than the other colors. Starting at the top, draw in accent veins on the side graining. Soften all over using the chip brush or a house painter's brush or softener.

**TIPS FROM THE PROS**

• The glaze should be transparent, adding just a haze of color.
• If any portion of the side grain seems too dark to you, lightly drag out the accent color with the chip brush or a soft rag.

**15** Starting at the top, drag the fan brush or veiner down the side graining to sharpen up some of the veining and break up any thick, dark lines of paint.

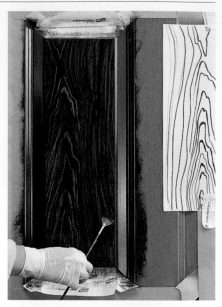

**TIPS FROM THE PROS**

• Hold the brush at an angle; the whole width doesn't have to press against the surface.

**16** Soften with the softener or a house painter's brush. To darken the veins, sweep the brush in horizontal strokes; to lighten them, sweep in vertical strokes.

**17** Remove any tape. Clean all equipment. Let the graining dry overnight. If there are other areas of your item to be grained, take each to this stage before proceeding.

**18** Squeeze a small amount of each artist's oil onto your palette. Measure out 6 tablespoons of medium #2 into a tuna can and add 3 to 4 drops of japan drier. Dip a clean chip brush into the medium and then pick up some of each color. Brush the surface all over in an up and down fashion. Soften with the same brush.

**TIPS FROM THE PROS**

• The glaze should be transparent, adding just a haze of color.
• Make this toning glaze variously redder or browner as you like by picking up more of one color oil or another.

**19** With a paper towel, wipe away the glaze from some parts of the pattern to bring out highlights.

**20** Hold the chip brush at a 45° angle to the surface. Using a series of short, interrupted strokes, pull the brush down through the glaze on part of the side grain, creating a ladder pattern of dark undulations. Then soften with the same brush.

**21** To create cross pores, hold the same chip brush sideways and press the middle part of the bristles onto darker areas where there are no undulations.

**22** If there are other areas of your item to be grained, take each to this stage before proceeding. Let each dry.

**23** Varnish the grained surface to intensify the color and protect the painting.

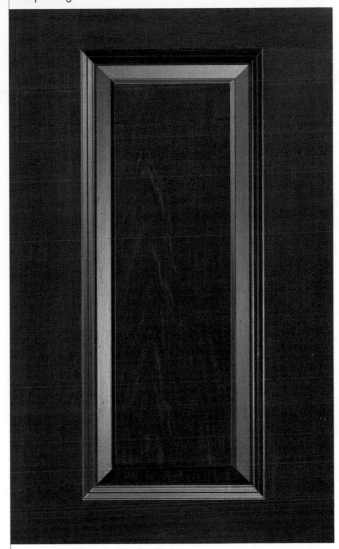

# KNOTTY PINE

## ADDITIONAL TOOLS

¹/₂" short-bristled artist's brush
Two 3" chip brushes
Script liner (brush)
Veiner (brush)
Curved painter's tool with
   comb edge
Foam brush
3" house painter's brush or
   softener (brush)

## BASE COAT

Latex satin paint, creamy
   yellow

## MEDIUM #1

Acrylic satin medium, as
   needed
Small amount of gel retarder

## MEDIUM #2

1 part linseed oil
1 part thinner
Japan drier

## ARTIST'S TUBE ACRYLICS

Titanium white
Raw sienna
Burnt sienna

## ARTIST'S OILS

Yellow ochre
Raw sienna
Burnt sienna

## FINISHES

3-lb cut amber shellac
Denatured alcohol
Low-luster to semigloss varnish,
   as desired

---

**1** Apply the base coat and let it dry, 2 days for latex, 2–3 days for alkyd. Lightly sand. Wipe with a tack cloth.

---

**2** Sketch out your grain pattern on a piece of paper of roughly the same proportions as the area to be grained.

### TIPS FROM THE PROS

• You'll need a different pattern for each principal section. Narrow sections such as rails and stiles can have simple straight graining, for which no pattern is necessary, or can be figured, as is the left stile in the photos.

---

**3** Squeeze out a small amount of the acrylic white, raw sienna, and burnt sienna onto your palette. Place a drop of gel retarder on top of each color. With the palette knife, mix the colors together. Place a tablespoon of acrylic satin medium on your palette and blend it with a drop of retarder.

---

**4** Dip the short-bristled brush into the medium and then pick up some of the mixed paint; blend on the palette. Begin drawing the peaks of the heart grain, working from the bottom up and using a sketchy motion to add depth as well as width at the top of each peak. After you've drawn a few peaks, soften with

a chip brush, starting at the bottom and working upward.

### TIPS FROM THE PROS

• Reload your brush as necessary.
• If the glaze is too thick and won't move on the surface, add a drop of water.
• If your sketched peaks point down, reverse the directions and work from the top down.
• The softening should stretch the glaze, making the peak veins more realistic.
• The acrylic glaze will dry quickly, so soften promptly and often.
• You can wipe off a painted line at any time. Wrap a paper towel around your finger and rub off the portion you don't like. If the paint has dried, just rub harder.

---

**5** With the short-bristled brush, extend the sides of each peak toward the bottom. Work from the lowest peak up. Keep a little space between the veins but don't let the pattern grow progressively wider as it works downward.

**6** Refer to your sketch and determine where the center of a knot, if there is one, will fall. With the script liner, paint a small irregular oval for the knot center. Paint in a delicate peaked vein above the knot and then another below the knot, connecting the two. Add another peaked vein above the knot.

**7** Continue in this manner to make concentric veins around the knot.

**8** Change to the short-bristled brush and add more veins above and then below the knot, sketching in the peaks as before. Soften vertically with the chip brush, moving the brush up or down from the center of the knot.

**9** Referring to steps 3 and 4 and your sketch, complete this section of heart grain. Mask any adjacent areas before continuing.

**10** With the veiner, pick up some of the mixed acrylic paint on your palette and also some acrylic medium. Run the comb edge of the painter's tool through the veiner to separate the bristles.

**TIPS FROM THE PROS**

• If the paint seems too thick, dip the veiner in water and rub it on the palette.

**11** Starting at the top, lightly drag the veiner next to the heart-grain patterns to create side grain. Repeat to fill in as necessary. Then let the graining dry.

**TIPS FROM THE PROS**

• If you are veining a panel, rotate your wrist as you drag the sides so the veins fall on the molding as well as the recess.

• Rotate your wrist as you fill narrow areas—this will compress the bristles and make the veins closer and denser.

## STAINING A KNOT

• The grain of real pine sometimes has a dark area, as if it were stained or dyed. You can easily add this feature to your work. Let the veins dry first. For the stain on the stile to the left of our panel, we used equal amounts of raw and burnt sienna; you can vary the color as you wish.

1. Referring to step 12, seal the component to which you'd like to add a stain. This will allow you to wipe off the stain if you don't like it.

2. Mix equal parts of artist's acrylic and acrylic satin medium (straight, not medium #1); blend in an amount of gel retarder equal to no more than 20% of the mixture.

3. Brush this wash over the graining where desired. Let it dry.

**12** Remove any tape. If there are other areas of your item to be grained, take each to this stage before proceeding. Clean all equipment.

**13** To seal the surface, mix equal parts of denatured alcohol and 3-lb cut shellac; apply the mixture with a foam brush. Let it dry.

**14** Pour 3 tablespoons of medium #2 into a tuna can. Add 3 drops of japan drier. Squeeze a small amount of each artist's oil onto your palette. Dip a clean chip brush into the medium and then pick up some of each color paint and apply it to the surface in a straight up and down fashion. Soften with the 3" house painter's brush or softener.

### TIPS FROM THE PROS

• The glaze should be transparent, adding just a haze of color.

• Use more burnt sienna for a mellower tone.

• You can add more color to selected areas and soften again to create subtle variations.

**15** To create highlights, remove the glaze between some of the veins in the heart grain with a wadded paper towel. Then soften with the paintbrush.

**16** With a paper towel, wipe off a small dot on each side of the knot. Place the paintbrush above the knot and drag it toward the knot, forming a "smile" in the glaze. Then drag a "frown" up from below the knot. Then soften with the same brush. (The frown is in progress in the photo.)

**17** Hold a clean 3" chip brush at a 45° angle to the surface. Using a series of short, interrupted strokes, pull the brush down through the glaze on part of the side grain, creating a ladder pattern of dark undulations. Then soften with the same brush.

**18** To create cross pores, hold the chip brush sideways and press the middle part of the bristles onto starker areas where there are no undulations. Let the paint dry.

**19** If there are other areas of your item to be grained, take each to this stage before proceeding.

**20** Varnish the grained surface to intensify the color and protect the painting. Use a tinted or clear varnish, as you wish.

*The graining on this door is a fantasy interpretation of exotic woods, painted using Burl and Knotty Pine techniques and trompe l'oeil panels. The door frame is an imaginary stone created with a combination of Marble and Sponging techniques.*

**M**arble is an eccentrically patterned stone. Re-creating it requires some skill and judgment but is not as challenging as you might think. Marble is often used for mantels, moldings, and tile; faux marble can be painted on fluted or other relief surfaces. Before you begin a project, spend some time observing the veining and color variations of real marble (photos are fine). Here we demonstrate two kinds of marble—Yellow Sienna and Bleu Belge (black with white veins).

*Right: White faux marbling brings out the lavish detail of the moldings, mantelpiece, and alcoves.*
*Below: Warm beige marbling highlights the statuesque moldings and pilasters framing these oversized windows.*
*Bottom: Painted faux marble tiles, in subtle hues and complete with contrasting insets, give an elegant finish to a plain floor.*

## TOOLS

Paint tray and brushes or roller for base coat
Latex gloves
Sandpaper: 220–400 grit
Tack cloth
Painter's masking tape
Empty, clean tuna can
Artist's palette
3/8" round short-haired hog bristle artist's brush (2 for Yellow Marble)
1" flat artist's brush (for Bleu Belge Marble)
Paper towels or rags
Two 3" chip brushes (3–4 for Yellow Marble)
House painter's brush (optional, for softening)
Spatter stick

## MEDIUM

1 part linseed oil
1 part thinner
Japan drier (added later)

## FINISH

Satin or semigloss varnish, as desired (use mineral spirit soluble acrylic varnish if you marble in oil paint)

## For Yellow Sienna
### BASE COAT

Latex or alkyd satin paint, pale creamy yellow

### ARTIST'S OILS

Titanium white
Yellow ochre
Raw sienna
Burnt sienna
Raw umber
Ivory black

## For Bleu Belge
### BASE COAT

Latex or alkyd satin or eggshell paint, black

### ARTIST'S OILS

Titanium white
Yellow ochre

*Before you begin, read Basics, pages 7–39. Also read Spattering, pages 72–75. To marble with artist's acrylics, read About Glazes and Washes, page 15.*

*Immediately submerge oil- or solvent-soiled rags in water. Discard according to local ordinances.*

## TIPS FOR MARBLE

• If you are marbling an object such as a mantel or a column, work from the top down. Complete all the steps through spattering (and subsequent softening) on each section before proceeding to the adjacent section. Use common sense about masking adjacent areas and be sure to remove the tape whenever you stop to let the paint dry.

• Clean up at the end of each day and prepare additional medium and paint as needed.

• To paint marble tiles, refer to Stripes and Grids, pages 84–85, to tape a grid on your surface. Don't carry the veins or any directional shading from one tile to another. For a checkerboard pattern, mask alternate squares.

# YELLOW SIENNA MARBLE

**1** Apply the base coat and let it dry, 2 days for latex, 2–3 days for alkyd. Lightly sand with sandpaper. Wipe with a tack cloth.

**2** Pour about 2 tablespoons of the medium into the tuna can and add 2 drops of japan drier. Squeeze a little bit of white, yellow ochre, raw sienna, and burnt sienna artist's oils onto your palette. With a chip brush, pick up a small amount of the medium, then some of each color, and mix loosely on your palette.

**3** Lightly brush the glaze onto the surface in a crisscross fashion. To make some areas lighter and some darker, vary the proportions of the colors picked up with the brush.

**4** Soften by whisking the same brush over the surface.

**5** While the yellow glaze is still wet, dip a second chip brush into the medium and then into the white artist's oil and brush haphazardly onto some of the lighter portions of the yellow glaze. With the first chip brush, blend in the white, creating a cloudlike effect and establishing a directional pattern.

**6** Dip the ³/₈" artist's brush into the medium and then pick up some yellow ochre, raw sienna, and a tiny bit of white. Loosely sketch in veins to outline some lighter and darker yellow areas. Hold the brush low on the handle to keep the strokes loose.

## TIPS FROM THE PROS

• Make thicker veins along some portions of the darker areas.
• Some of the veins should form irregular and lozenge shapes; some should run at opposing angles. No one direction should be dominant.

**7** Whisk the first chip brush over the veining to soften. If any part of the pattern seems harsh, pounce out the area with the tips of the bristles. Pounce between some of the veins on the darker areas, then soften minimally.

## TIPS FROM THE PROS

• To give the surface a little more depth, pick up some of the veining colors (but none of the medium) with the chip brush and pounce in between the veins in the yellow areas.

**8** Squeeze a little black and raw umber artist's oils onto the palette; dip the previously used artist's brush into the medium and pick up some of each. Very lightly sketch in more veins, forming an irregular network.

## TIPS FROM THE PROS

• Avoid creating obvious letter or number shapes—even though they occur in nature, they're not considered desirable.

• Yellow Sienna marble is sometimes heavily veined, and sometimes hardly veined at all. You can put in as much veining as you like, and place more in some areas than in others.

**9** Soften with the third chip brush, brushing in the direction of the strongest vein.

**10** With the clean ³/₈" artist's brush, pick up a small amount of medium and some white and yellow ochre artist's oils, and dot into some of the shapes to accent them. Then do the same with raw sienna and yellow ochre.

**11** Add more veins if you wish. Soften with a clean chip brush or with a house painter's brush.

**12** Complete the marbling to this stage on all portions of your object before proceeding with the next step. It is not necessary for the paint to dry before you continue.

**13** Dip a clean chip brush into the medium and then into the white artist's oil; mix on the palette. Spatter on, concentrating the spatters in the lighter parts of the marble. Soften with the first chip brush, whisking it across the area in a crisscross fashion. Spatter again, this time using raw sienna and yellow ochre and concentrating on the darker areas.

**14** Soften immediately with the chip brush or house painter's brush used in step 11. Let the paint dry completely.

## TIPS FROM THE PROS

• At this point you can repeat any of the steps to add more detail. Or if you feel a portion of your marble has become too white, add a little of the base color or the yellow glazes over it and retouch the veins if necessary.

**15** Varnish the marbled surface to protect it and give it a realistic sheen. You can see that we muted some of the brighter white areas with yellow before finishing this mantel.

# BLEU BELGE (BLACK) MARBLE

**1** Apply the base coat and let it dry, 2 days for latex, 2–3 days for alkyd. Lightly sand. Wipe with a tack cloth.

**2** Pour 2 tablespoons of the medium into the tuna can. Dip a paper towel into the medium and wipe it over the area to be marbled. Add 2 drops of japan drier to the medium in the can.

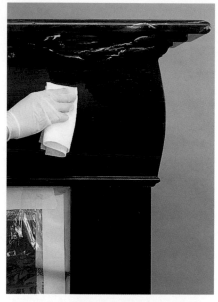

**3** Squeeze a little bit of each oil onto your palette. Dip the $^3/_8$" round artist's brush into the medium and then take up some titanium white and mix with a little yellow ochre on the palette. Very lightly sketch in veins, moving in a lateral direction. Hold the brush low on the handle to keep the strokes loose.

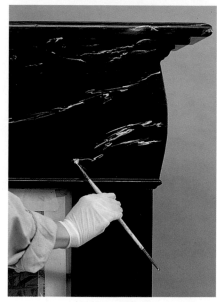

**TIPS FROM THE PROS**

• Keep the veins moving in the same general direction, spacing them at irregular intervals. The veins should not be perfectly parallel, and they should trail off rather than end abruptly.

• Reload the brush only when it becomes dry; this will create veins that are more intense in some areas than in others. Be sure to always dip the brush into the medium before dipping it into and mixing additional oil color.

• If you pick up too much medium (so that the brush is saturated), blot the brush on a paper towel.

**4** Soften the veining by lightly whisking a chip brush across the surface in the same lateral direction.

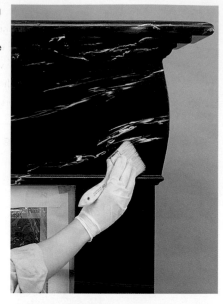

**5** Using the 1" flat artist's brush, scumble on (rub on) a clump of the mixed white and yellow ochre paint between two veins.

**6** Immediately scumble this paint clump with the chip brush, rubbing it into the surface until it makes a very faint cloud.

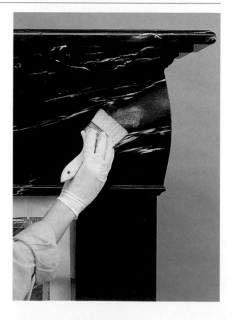

**7** Repeat steps 5 and 6 as appropriate to your surface.

**8** With the ³/₈" round brush, sketch occasional vertical veins to bisect the lateral veins. These veins should not be precisely parallel nor identical.

**9** Soften the veins with the chip brush. Stand back and look at the marble. Add more veins if you wish.

**10** Dip a clean chip brush into the medium and then into the white artist's oil; mix on the palette. Spatter on, concentrating the spatters in the emptier parts of the marble.

**11** Soften with the first chip brush.

**12** Complete the marbling to this stage on all portions of your object before proceeding with the next step. Let the paint dry completely, at least overnight.

**13** Tone the veins to add depth: Dilute a small amount of black base paint with medium or water, as appropriate, making it nearly transparent; use the artist's brush and mix on your palette. Then, with the same brush, sketch the diluted paint very lightly over some portions of the veins. Let dry.

### TIPS FROM THE PROS

• Alternatively, you can dilute any brown hue artist's oil or acrylic to make this toning glaze.

**14** Varnish the marbled surface to protect it and give it a realistic sheen.

**M**alachite is a semiprecious stone with a distinctive swirled pattern. Faux malachite looks impressive but is fairly easy to paint—you simply drag a piece of torn cardboard through a wet glaze, incising curved wavy lines characteristic of the stone. Malachite is traditionally used to decorate small, flat surfaces, such as door panels, trays, and decorative boxes. It can be painted on smooth curved items, but the cardboard is difficult to maneuver on fluted or other relief surfaces.

## TOOLS

Paint tray and brush or roller for base coat
Latex gloves
Sandpaper: 220–400 grit
Tack cloth
Sketch paper
Painter's masking tape
Shiny lightweight cardboard
Empty, clean tuna can
Artist's palette
1¹/₂" foam (or flat artist's) brush
Touch-up or script liner brush
Pencil with eraser or eraser tool
2 chip brushes
Spatter stick
Paper towels or rags for cleanup

## BASE COAT

Alkyd or latex satin paint, pale blue-green

## MEDIUM

1 tablespoon linseed oil
1 tablespoon thinner
2 drops japan drier

## ARTIST'S OILS

2 parts indigo blue
2 parts cadmium green deep
1 part Ivory black

## FINISH

Low-luster to satin varnish, as desired

Before you begin, read Basics, pages 7–39. Also read Spattering, pages 72–75. Practice this technique first on paper (see page 19).

Immediately submerge oil- or solvent-soiled rags in water. Discard according to local ordinances.

## TIPS FOR MALACHITE

• Real malachite would be used in small pieces. To mimic its application, create an inlay pattern appropriate for the shape of the surface you're decorating.
• If you'd prefer a design with contrasting inlay lines, follow the directions for setting up Tortoiseshell on page 164.
• As you work, use common sense about masking adjacent areas and be sure to remove tape whenever you stop to let the paint dry. Touch up any seepage immediately.
• Clean up at the end of each day and prepare additional medium and paint as needed.

*Right: Despite its exuberant patterning, malachite has a subdued and refined demeanor, perfect for this serene decor.*
*Below: A bright navy and turquoise base adds modern pizzazz to a column masquerading as malachite.*
*Bottom: Silver is a natural companion for malachite—and a good choice for the complex portions of this obelisk.*

# MALACHITE

**1** Apply the base coat and let it dry, 2 days for latex, 2–3 days for alkyd. If you are working on an inset panel, prime or base coat the adjacent areas and let them dry. Lightly sand the malachite area and wipe it with the tack cloth.

**2** Plan a design with interlocking straight-edged sections on a piece of paper of roughly the same proportions as your surface. Before painting each section, you'll have to mask all its edges. You can paint as many nonadjacent sections at one time as you wish. After they are dry, you'll remask and paint the sections not painted the first time. Mark your sketch to indicate a plan for the first masking.

**TIPS FROM THE PROS**

• The more complex your design, the more difficult it will be to plan the masking, and the more drying steps you'll need. Try to set up a pattern in which every other section can be masked at one time. A good way to check this is to shade alternate sections; if two shaded sections abut, you won't be able to paint them in the same pass.

**3** Draw the design on your surface. Mask one or more nonadjacent shapes with tape. Press the tape firmly to prevent seepage.

**TIPS FROM THE PROS**

• If necessary, use scissors or a craft knife to cut the tape to conform to the marked design.

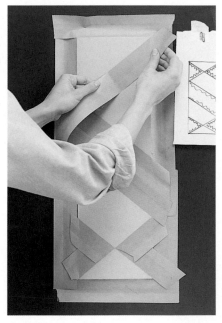

**4** Tear a small piece of cardboard to use as a painting tool. Don't try to make a clean tear; you want a deckle edge (rough edge) for your tool.

**TIPS FROM THE PROS**

• You can further tear the cardboard as you work, or tear other pieces, so don't worry if you don't know exactly what shape to start with.

• It won't matter whether the shiny or dull side of the cardboard faces up when you work; what will be important is that a deckle edge face the paint.

**5** Mix the medium in the tuna can. Squeeze a small amount of each of the artist's oils onto your palette. Dip the foam or artist's brush into the medium and then pick up equal amounts of the colors and mix them on your palette. Brush the glaze onto an exposed section of your surface.

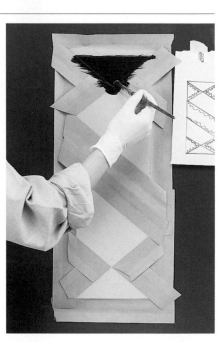

**TIPS FROM THE PROS**

• You can apply the glaze to more than one section if you like. If your exposed sections meet point to point, as do some of those shown, it's nearly impossible not to apply glaze to both, so spread the glaze completely over each.

**6** Holding the deckle edge down, gently drag the piece of cardboard over one section in a wavy or circular pattern. Wiggle the cardboard to make wavering lines.

**TIPS FROM THE PROS**

• If you don't like the pattern, brush out the glaze and try again.

• You don't have to stop right at the section edge; you can drag the cardboard onto the tape.

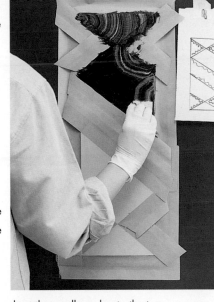

**7** Lift the cardboard. If you didn't fill the section with pattern, drag another pattern adjacent to the first. You can echo or extend the first pattern, or intersect it with another shape, but don't drag over it.

**TIPS FROM THE PROS**

• All the glaze should be patterned, with only the smallest gaps untouched by the cardboard.

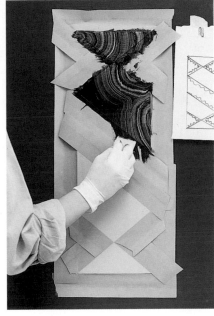

**8** To refine the pattern, touch up any areas where you think you've removed too much glaze. Use a touch-up brush dipped into the medium and then into the oils. If you wish to lighten an area, drag the edge of the pencil eraser or eraser tool through the glaze. Move your tool carefully between the dragged lines and try to echo their finesse.

**9** After all the exposed sections have been painted, remove the tape. Let the paint dry overnight.

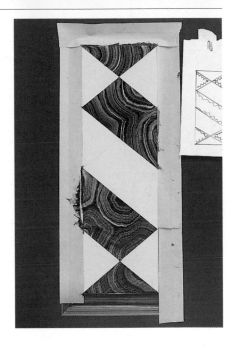

**10** Mask the next sections to be painted. Repeat steps 5–8. Continue in this way until the entire design has been painted. When all the sections have been painted, remove the tape and fill in any gaps between the sections with a touch-up brush dipped in medium and the artist's oils. Let the paint dry overnight.

**11** Dip a chip brush into the medium, then into the artist's oils. Lightly spatter the glaze over the design. Then lightly whisk a dry chip brush over the surface to soften the effect.

### TIPS FROM THE PROS

• If you've painted only a portion of your surface in a malachite pattern, be sure to mask the adjacent areas before you spatter.

**12** Varnish the malachite.

**13** If appropriate, finish painting the surrounding area, being sure to protect the malachite first.

**14** Note how we dragged the panel recess with the same glaze and used a blue-green black to paint the surrounding rails and stiles. For a different look, consider trimming a Malachite project with gold- or silver-leaf details.

In the past real tortoiseshell was often applied over colored silk, traditionally red, green, or ivory, which peeked through the transparent portions of the shell. We've chosen to demonstrate an inlaid pattern of tortoiseshell and ivory; the exposed background that simulates the ivory can be omitted. If you are a stickler for realism, bear in mind that tortoiseshell has always been a rare substance, available only in small pieces—a faux tortoiseshell wall would be faux indeed! Tortoiseshell is easy and quick to paint, but does have a couple of drying periods.

*Below: A mirror frame graced with faux tortoiseshell makes a wonderful companion for the exotic foliage hand-painted on the panel.*

*Bottom: While nature would never provide tortoiseshell pieces large enough to tile this floor, the fantasy checkerboard is fun, instantly elegant, and fairly easy to paint.*

### TOOLS

Paint tray and brush or roller for base coat
Latex gloves
Sandpaper: 220–400 grit
Tack cloth
1/8" masking tape
Painter's masking tape (optional)
Empty, clean tuna can
Artist's palette
1/2" flat artist's brush (or a paper towel)
3/8" round synthetic sable artist's brush
2" chip brush
Touch-up brush
Paper towels or rags for cleanup

### BASE

Latex semigloss paint, creamy yellow

### MEDIUM

1 tablespoon linseed oil
1 tablespoon thinner
2 drops japan drier

### ARTIST'S OILS

Burnt sienna
Burnt umber
Ivory black
Asphaltum (if unavailable, use the burnt umber)

### FINISH

Satin to semigloss varnish, as desired

*Before you begin, read Basics, pages 7–39. Practice this technique first on paper (see page 19). If you'd prefer to work in water-base paints, see About Glazes and Washes, page 15.*

*Immediately submerge oil- or solvent-soiled rags in water. Discard according to local ordinances.*

### TIPS FOR TORTOISESHELL

• Real tortoiseshell would be used in small pieces. To mimic its application, create an inlay pattern appropriate for the shape of the surface you're decorating. When you select a base color, remember that it will be exposed when you remove any inlay masking.

• If you'd prefer a design without exposed inlay lines, follow the directions for setting up Malachite, page 160. There is no need to divide a small surface.

• It's worth searching for narrow tape so that your inlay will be in proportion to the tortoiseshell (see the Tip on page 85).

• As you work, use common sense about masking adjacent areas and be sure to remove tape whenever you stop to let the paint dry. Touch up any seepage immediately.

• Clean up at the end of each day and prepare additional medium and paint as needed.

# TORTOISESHELL

**1** Apply the base coat and let it dry. If you are working on an inset panel, prime and base coat the adjacent areas and let them dry. Lightly sand the tortoiseshell area and wipe it with the tack cloth.

**2** Mark the inlay design, if using, and mask it with ⅛" tape. We masked diagonally crossed lines; we also masked the return edge of the raised panel. If appropriate, mask the edges adjacent to the area you'll be painting.

**3** Mix the medium in the tuna can. Squeeze a small amount of the burnt sienna, burnt umber, and black artist's oils onto your palette. Dip the ½" flat artist's brush or a wadded-up piece of paper towel into the medium, then into the burnt sienna, and brush or rub over the entire surface.

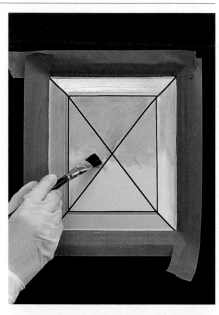

**4** Dip the ⅜" round artist's brush into the medium, then into the burnt sienna. Dot on the glaze; all the dots within a section should move in the same direction.

**TIPS FROM THE PROS**
• Don't make your dot pattern uniform. Instead, place the dots closer together in some areas than in others.
• For a more mottled pattern, make the dots more irregular and sometimes connected. We did this in the recess around the panel.
• To make the tortoiseshell look realistic, be sure some dots run off the edges of each section, but not onto other sections.

**5** Dip the ⅜" round artist's brush into the medium, then into the burnt umber. Dab on dots either directly adjacent to or slightly overlapping the previous dots.

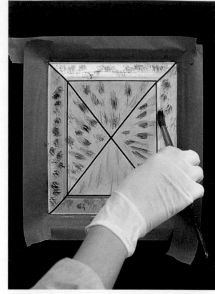

**6** Repeat, this time using the black artist's oil.

**TIPS FROM THE PROS**
• You can intensify the mottled effect by smearing the black glaze slightly.
• Sections of mottled tortoiseshell should be more densely covered.

**7** Soften the effect by lightly stroking the chip brush over the surface in the direction of the dots.

**TIPS FROM THE PROS**
• You can add more of any of the three colors at this point. Soften again after applying.

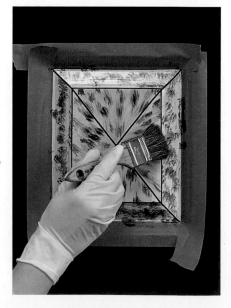

**8** Dip the ³/₈" round artist's brush into the medium and then into the burnt sienna. Dab on tiny specks of color throughout. Then soften again with the chip brush.

**9** Remove the tape. Touch up any seepage. Let the paint dry overnight.

**10** Retape the design. Squeeze some asphaltum or burnt umber artist's oil onto the palette. Dip the round brush into the medium, then into the paint, and brush together on the palette to make a thin wash. Paint the tortoiseshell surface with this wash.

**TIPS FROM THE PROS**

• You can use any small brush for this step; a foam brush or chip brush would be fine.

**11** Using a touch-up brush, add more black dots if you wish.

**12** Soften with the chip brush. Remove the tape and touch up if necessary. Let the paint dry overnight.

**13** Retape and then apply the varnish. If appropriate, finish painting the surrounding area, being sure to protect the tortoiseshell first.

**14** The varnish deepens the tortoiseshell colors and makes the effect quite realistic. Here the black rails and stiles have been varnished to further set off the rich colors.

Gilt details imbue architectural elements with elegance and sophistication. There are numerous products for adding a metal finish, including paint, powder, and cream mediums. Leafing is one of the prettiest, with tiny irregular ridges where the leaves overlap distinguishing it from other gilding techniques. Leaf should always be applied over a painted surface. Warm-hue metals work best over a warm yellow, brown, or red background; silver can be effective over a cool background; and both work next to white or black. You can apply leaf to a flat or modeled surface, covering it entirely or partially as you prefer.

Here we explain gilding with composition metal leaf rather than real gold—the composition metal is readily available, inexpensive, and easy to work with, and its bright finish can be antiqued with an aging glaze. Its only drawback is that over time it will tarnish.

*Right: Gold-leaf embellishments paired with distressed woodwork and fantasy marbling evoke an undocumented but appealing era of antiquity.*
*Below: Copper, gold, and silver leafing adorn this magnificent molding, set effectively against sponged-off walls and a stenciled ceiling.*
*Bottom: A striking gold-leafed wall, finished with an antiquing glaze, reflects the sunshine streaming down this staircase. Though perhaps a daunting project for those with limited time or funds, this treatment could be scaled back and still be appealing.*

## TOOLS

3" brown paper painter's tape
Latex gloves
Mixing containers
Stir sticks
Small paintbrush for primer
Foam brushes
1/2" flat synthetic artist's brush
Mottler (small, soft brush)
Small aluminum or plastic container
Small stencil brush or chip brush
Cotton balls
Touch-up brush
1/2" round nylon artist's brush
Paper towels or rags for cleanup

## PRIMER

If needed, as appropriate for your surface

## BASE COAT

Any satin or high-gloss paint (gloss is better if gilding will not be antiqued)

## LEAF

Composition metal leaf
Water-base or quick-drying oil-base size

### For antiquing
## ADDITIONAL TOOLS

Artist's palette
Empty, clean tuna can

## ARTIST'S OILS

Cassel earth
Burnt umber
Van Dyke brown

## MEDIUM

1 tablespoon linseed oil
1 tablespoon paint thinner
2 drops japan drier

## SEALER (OPTIONAL)

Satin oil-base varnish or mineral soluble acrylic varnish

*We used deep Chinese red artist's acrylic for the base coat.*

*Before you begin, read Basics, pages 7–39.*

*Immediately submerge oil- or solvent-soiled rags in water. Discard according to local ordinances.*

# GILDING

## TIPS FOR GILDING

- Size is a type of adhesive. You'll find it with other gilding supplies at art and craft supply stores.
- Use common sense to select foam paintbrushes in a size appropriate for the modeling of the surface you are painting.
- Keep the metal leaf sandwiched between two sheets of tissue when you handle it.
- If you're gilding a relief surface, use scissors to cut the leaf into strips slightly longer than the longest contour before you begin.
- If you are antiquing a large gilded area, mix more medium as necessary, or premix Oil Medium #2 (page 18), adding 2 drops of drier to every 2 tablespoons of the mixture when ready to use.

**1** If necessary, mask areas adjacent to the surface that will be gilded. Using a paintbrush, apply the primer to the entire surface and let it dry. Then, using the foam brush, apply the base coat to the entire surface, tapping the paint into any crevices and smoothing any bubbles. Let the paint dry. Repeat if necessary.

**2** Using the ¹/₂" flat artist's brush, apply the size to the areas you wish to gild. If you are using oil-base size, apply a thin layer and check that coverage is even. Be careful not to get the size on any adjacent areas. Let the size dry until it's slightly tacky but not sticky.

### TIPS FROM THE PROS

- Touching the size with your fingertips can compromise its adhesive quality. To test for tackiness, touch lightly with your knuckle.

**3** Pick up a piece of leaf sandwiched between tissues and hold it between your thumb and forefinger. Slide the leaf forward so that it extends slightly beyond the tissues, then slide the bottom tissue back. Hold the leaf over the surface.

### TIPS FROM THE PROS

- When you apply leaf to cover a solid area such as the center of this medallion, begin at the perimeter of the area and work toward the center.

**4** Slide the bottom tissue out completely and lower the leaf onto the surface. To secure the leaf, pat the top tissue against it with the forefinger of your other hand.

**5** Continue to apply the leaf, adding each piece so that it slightly overlaps the previous piece. Where there is no size, any extending large pieces of leaf may tear off as you work. You can add them to the surface as you go or set them aside.

**6** Pounce the leafed surface with the mottler to make sure the leaf adheres tightly.

**7** Fill any gaps in the leafed areas, gently tearing off overhanging pieces and then positioning them with the mottler or your fingers.

**8** Use the small stencil brush to rub the leaf more tightly onto the surface and at the same time brush off any loose pieces, catching them in the small container.

**TIPS FROM THE PROS**

• If you've inadvertently put size in an area you didn't want to gild, remove the unwanted leaf with a cotton swab dipped in a little paint thinner.

**9** Rub the leafed areas with a dry cotton ball to smooth out any wrinkles.

**10** To patch any remaining gaps, carefully apply size to them with the touch-up brush and let them dry until slightly tacky. Then fill the gaps with leaf scraps from the container. Pounce them with the soft brush and smooth with a cotton ball. If necessary, touch up the exposed base coat with more paint. Let the gilding dry overnight.

**TIPS FROM THE PROS**

• How completely you fill the gaps is really a matter of preference. Some people like to leave bits of the background peeking through the gilding, especially if they intend to antique it.

**11** Using the round nylon artist's brush, brush around all the grooves to remove any loose bits of metal leaf.

**12** At this point the gilding is complete and brilliant. You can stop at this stage if you want the gilding to stay bright or you can antique it, following steps 13 and 14 on the next page.

**TIPS FROM THE PROS**

• The composition metal will stay bright for several years, but eventually it will tarnish. If you wish, you can add a coat of low-luster varnish to prevent discoloration.

**13** If you'd like to antique the gilding, apply an aging glaze as follows. Mix the medium in the tuna can. Squeeze a small amount of each artist's oil onto the palette. Dip the round nylon artist's brush into the medium, then pick up some of each color and mix on the palette. Brush the glaze over the entire surface, covering the gilded and painted areas completely.

### TIPS FROM THE PROS

• If too much glaze accumulates in any of the grooves or the glaze seems too heavy, you can pounce it out with a stencil brush or chip brush.

• If you think the glaze is too dark, wipe it off while it is still wet and try a different proportion of colors.

**14** The aging glaze dulls the gold and deepens the color of the paint, mellowing the overall effect. If you wish, you can add a coat of low-luster varnish to prevent discoloration.

*Gold leaf combines with fantasy stone, sponged-off walls, and dragged and stenciled woodwork to create an upbeat, eclectic, and thoroughly modern environment.*

When copper oxidizes, a patina of green deposits, or verdigris, forms on its surface. Faux verdigris imparts an aura of antiquity to architectural metalwork and accessories, especially those that might once have lived in a garden. Strictly speaking, verdigris should be applied only to objects that might have been made from copper, but the effect is often used on other metals and all sorts of accessories. Because commercially available kits quickly replicate verdigris (and several other aging patinas), there is no need to follow the traditional method of painting subtle layers of glaze. Each kit works a little differently; refer to our directions as a general guide but be sure follow your kit manufacturer's directions.

*Below: Verdigris finishes need not be reserved for sculptural objects—and the fact that you're unlikely to run across copper tiles is no reason not to create a facsimile. Here, below a colorwashed and lightly sponged wall, the verdigris conceals everyday plastic tiles. The sunflower sculpture and the lamps also have touches of verdigris, and the étagère has a patina of true age.*

## TOOLS

3" brown paper painter's tape
Latex gloves
Mixing containers
Stir sticks
Small paintbrush for primer
$^1/_2$" flat or round artist's brushes

## PRIMER

As appropriate for your surface

## PAINT

Commercial verdigris kit with copper base coat and patina top coat

## TIPS FOR VERDIGRIS

• Most verdigris kits work on numerous surfaces—metal, wood, plaster, even plastic—as long as they are properly primed. The medallion used in the sample is cast resin and was already primed when purchased. Refer to your verdigris kit to select the proper primer.

• Use common sense to select paintbrushes in a size appropriate to the modeling of the surface you are painting.

• It is not always clear from the kit whether the verdigris system is water or oil base; test a small amount to see if water cleanup is feasible. You might want to use disposable or inexpensive brushes.

# VERDIGRIS

**1** If necessary, mask areas adjacent to the surface you'll be painting. Apply the primer to the surface with a small paintbrush. Let it dry.

**2** With an artist's brush (or a clean foam brush), apply the copper base coat. Let it dry as directed on the product label.

**3** Apply a second coat of the copper base coat. Wait just a few minutes before proceeding.

**4** When the surface becomes tacky but not dry, apply the patina top coat with a clean artist's brush. The top coat is clear and it doesn't change color immediately.

### TIPS FROM THE PROS

• The top coat is thin and runny. While you can't really predict the way the copper will react, the green patina tends to be more intense wherever the top coat collects, so you can influence the results by letting the drips flow naturally or brushing them out.

**5** After about 30 minutes the top coat will have reacted with the base coat, causing the copper paint to oxidize into the familiar green patina.

### TIPS FROM THE PROS

• At this time you can add more of the top coat to specific areas to intensify the patina.

• If you feel some portions of the surface are too plain, you can also reapply the base coat to them selectively, let it become tacky, and then apply more top coat.

*The verdigris finish brings out the lovely curved leaf design
on this sconce—one of the many cast-resin architectural
embellishments available at paint and home stores.*

# INDEX

Note: Page numbers in *italic* refer to Tricks of the Trade; those in **bold** indicate a photograph.

# PHOTOGRAPHY CREDITS

## PHOTOGRAPHERS

Richard Bryant/ARCAID: 92 bottom inset, 98 bottom inset. **Mark Darley/ESTO:** 47, 50. **Phillip Ennis:** 37 top, 46 top inset, 55 top inset, 57 right, 59 bottom inset, 62 bottom right, 66 top inset, 77, 81, 98, 105 bottom right, 111 top, 127 bottom left, 152 top inset, 163 bottom inset, 166 top inset, 167. **Ron Forth:** 63 bottom inset, 120 inset, 153. **Tria Giovan:** 46 bottom inset, 116–17, 123 right. **Jeff Goldberg/ESTO:** 80 bottom inset. **John M. Hall:** 43, 55 bottom inset, 71 bottom right, 103 right, 133. **Philip Harvey:** 167, 171 inset. **Dennis Krukowski:** 37 bottom, 38 top, 39, 41, 42 top inset, 83 bottom right, 86 top inset, 93, 109, 166 bottom inset. **Fred Lyon:** 59 top inset. **Richard Mandelkorn:** 51. **Steven Mays:** All step-by-step photos and pages 1, 53 right, 65 bottom, 72 inset, 73, 92 top inset, 112–13, 121, 128–29, 158 top inset, 159, 173. **E. Andrew McKinney:** 38 bottom, 76 top and bottom insets, 80 top inset, 87, 99, 125, 163 top inset, 166 top inset, 170 right. **Melabee M. Miller:** 106. **Bradley Olman:** 42 bottom inset, 86 bottom inset, 107, 111 bottom, 138 bottom inset. **Robert Perron:** 66 bottom inset, 132 inset. **Paul Rocheleau:** 139. **Eric Roth:** 151 right. **JoAnn Masaoka Van Atta:** 67. **Brian Vanden Brink:** 97. **Vigini Studio:** 63 top inset. **The Terry Wild Studio:** 152 bottom inset, 158 bottom inset. **Marilyn "Angel" Wynn:** 124 inset.

## DECORATIVE PAINTERS AND INTERIOR DESIGNERS

All step-by-step samples painted by Justina Jorrin Barnard/Peinture Decorative, New York City. **Page 1:** Decorative painter, Justina Jorrin Barnard. **37 bottom:** Interior design, Jeffrey Lincoln & Associates. **38 top:** Decorative painter, Painted Decoration Studio. **38 bottom:** Decorative painter, Robert O'Conner Designs. Photo director, JoAnn Masaoka Van Atta. **39:** Interior design, Samuel Botero & Associates. Painting contractor, Simonson & Baric. **41:** Interior design, Ruthann Olsson. **42 top inset:** Decorative painter, Deborah Simon Decorative Painters. **43:** Interior design, Stephanie Stokes. **45 bottom:** Decorative painter, Gail Leddy. **46 top inset:** Interior design, Bonis-Mariotti & Associates. **46 bottom inset:** Decorative painter, Gail Leddy. **47:** Architect, Tucker & Marks. **51:** Interior design, Judith Ross & Company. **53 right, 55 top inset:** Decorative painter, Justina Jorrin Barnard. **59 top inset:** Architect, John C. Walker. **63 top inset:** Stencil design, Nicola Vigini/Vigini Studios; wall painted by Vandelae Studios. **63 bottom inset:** Decorative painter, Gary Lord/Gary Lord Wall Options. **65 bottom right:** Decorative painter, Justina Jorrin Barnard. **66 bottom inset:** Decorative painter, Robert Mintum Coale/Old World Finishes. **67:** Decorative painter, Peggy Del Rosario. Interior design, Lisa & Associates Interior Design. Photo director, JoAnn Masaoka Van Atta. **72 inset, 73:** Decorative painter, Justina Jorrin Barnard. **76 top inset:** Decorative painter, Carla Eagleton "Trump." Interior design, Sudie Woodson Interiors. Photo director, JoAnn Masaoka Van Atta. **76 bottom inset:** Decorative painter, Robert O'Conner Designs. Photo director, JoAnn Masaoka Van Atta. **77:** Decorative painter, James Allen Smith. Interior design, Gary Crain. **80 top inset:** Interior design, Elizabeth Hill/Selby House. Photo director, JoAnn Masaoka Van Atta. **80 bottom inset:** Architect, Chad Floyd/Centerbrook. **81 bottom right:** Interior design, Gail Green. **83 bottom right:** Decorative painters, Lillian Bingham, Katie Scott Rosenshein/Paintrix. Interior design, Threadneedle Street of Montclair. **86 top inset:** Interior design, Michael Lane. **87:** Decorative painter, Erik Seniska. Photo director, JoAnn Masaoka Van Atta. **92 top inset:** Decorative painter, Justina Jorrin Barnard. **92 bottom inset:** Thematic House, Architect, Charles Jencks. **93:** Interior design, Ruthann Olsson. **97:** Photographed at Norlands Living History Center, Livermore, Maine. **98 top inset:** Interior design, Barbara Ostrom & Associates. **98 bottom inset:** Photographed at Carl Larsson House, Sweden. Decorative painter, Carl Larsson. **99:** Decorative painter, The Master's Touch. Interior design, Dominique Sanchot Stenzel/La Belle France. Photo director, JoAnn Masaoka Van Atta. **103 right:** Decorative painter, Andy Holland. **105 bottom right:** Interior design, Saunders & Walsh. **106:** Decorative painter, Sandy D'Almeida. Interior design, Linda & Richard Kregloski. **107:** Interior design, Bonnie Pressley/Decorating Den. **109:** Interior design, H.A. Fields Design Studio. **111 top:** Decorative painter, James Allen Smith. **111 bottom:** Decorative painter, Deborah Darnell. **112 insets, 113:** Decorative painter, Justina Jorrin Barnard. **116 insets, 117:** Decorative painter, Gail Leddy. **120 inset:** Decorative painter, Gary Lord/Gary Lord Wall Options. **121:** Decorative painter, Justina Jorrin Barnard. **123 right:** Decorative painter, Gail Leddy. **125:** Decorative painter, Carla Eagleton "Trump." Interior design, Lisa DeLong, DeLong Designs & Interiors. Photo director, JoAnn Masaoka Van Atta. **127 bottom left:** Interior design, Samuel Botero & Associates. **128 inset, 129:** Decorative painter, Justina Jorrin Barnard. **132 inset:** Decorative painter, Michele Raiti. Interior design, Jennifer Walker, ASID. Architects, Johnson & Michalsen Architects. **133:** Interior design, Stephanie Stokes. **138 inset:** Interior design, Jan Tomlinson/Decorating Den. **139:** Photographed at Mount Vernon. **151 right:** Interior design, Charles Spada. **152 top inset:** Interior design, Gail Whiting Design Consultants. **152 bottom inset:** Decorative painter, Margaret Bierman. **153:** Decorative painter, Gary Lord/Gary Lord Wall Options. **158 top inset:** Decorative painter, Justina Jorrin Barnard. **158 bottom inset:** Decorative painter, Margaret Bierman. **159:** Decorative painter, Justina Jorrin Barnard. **163 top inset:** Decorative painter, Samantha Renko. Interior design, Frank Van Duerm Design Associates. Photo director, JoAnn Masaoka Van Atta. **163 bottom inset:** Interior design, Richard Neas. **166 top inset:** Decorative painter, Robert O'Conner Designs. Photo director, JoAnn Masaoka Van Atta. **166 bottom inset:** Interior design, Suzanne O'Connell. Architect, Donald Carruthers. **167:** Decorative painter, Peggy Del Rosario. Photo director, JoAnn Masaoka Van Atta. **170 right:** Decorative painter, Robert O'Conner Designs. Photo director, JoAnn Masaoka Van Atta. **171 inset:** Decorative painter, Peggy Del Rosario. Photo director, JoAnn Masaoka Van Atta. **173:** Decorative painter, Justina Jorrin Barnard.